Ireland In The

The Irish Insurrectic
Set In Its Context Of The World War

by

Charles James O'Donnell
(1849-1934)

and

Brendan Clifford

Athol Books
10 Athol Street
Belfast
BT12 4GX

Also by Brendan Clifford

Connolly: The Polish Aspect (pamphlet)
Connolly Cut-Outs: *A Review Of Some Caricatures Of James Connolly* (pamphlet)
Derry And The Boyne: A Contemporary Account Of The Siege Of Derry, The Battle
Of The Boyne and the General Condition of Ireland in The Jacobite War by Nicholas
Plunket (Introduction: Brendan Clifford)
The Life And Poems Of Thomas Moore
Belfast In The French Revolution
The Veto Controversy (including Thomas Moore's "A Letter To The Roman
Catholics Of Dublin, 1810)
The Dubliner: The Lives, Times & Writings Of James Clarence Mangan
Thomas Russell And Belfast (a biography of "the man from God knows where", the
Munster soldier who was central to the social life of Belfast in the United Irish phase,
and was executed for his part in Emmet's Rebellion)

Introductions to three collections of writings by United Irishmen: W.S. Dickson,
James Porter and T.L. Birch

Ireland In The Great War
The Irish Insurrection Of 1916
Set In Its Context Of The World War
by
Charles James O'Donnell
(1849-1934)
and
Brendan Clifford
ISBN 0 85034 055 1

is published by
Athol Books,
10 Athol Street,
Belfast,
BT12 4GX.

© Athol Books 1992

This book is sold subject to the condition that it shall not, by way of trade or otherwise,
be lent, resold, hired out, or otherwise circulated without the publisher's prior consent
in any form of binding or cover other than that in which it is published and without a
similar condition including this condition being imposed on the subsequent purchaser.

Contents

INTRODUCTION

"The two supreme services which Ireland rendered Great Britain are her accession to the allied cause on the outbreak of the Great War and her withdrawal from the House of Commons at its close." (Churchill, quoted by C.J. O'Donnell.)

The first World War was the major military event in the life of the Irish nation during the past three hundred years, and it was the event in which the independent Irish state originated. It is, therefore, remarkable that amidst all the publishing done in nationalist Ireland there does not seem to be a single history of that great war—which was once called the Great War and ought still to be so called—to which Ireland contributed 200,000 soldiers.

The Liberal-Imperialist Government of the United Kingdom declared war on Germany on August 4th, 1914. John Redmond, the leader of the major Irish Party, the Home Rule Party, supported the British declaration of war. The Liberal-Imperialist Prime Minister, Herbert Henry Asquith, addressed a great war rally in Dublin on September 25th, 1914. His speech was issued as a penny pamphlet under the title **A United Empire**. A speech delivered by Asquith in Edinburgh a week earlier, on September 18th, was also issued as a penny pamphlet. Its title was **The War Of Civilisation**. That title summed up the pretended object of the UK Government in the war. The means by which that object was to be achieved was the destruction of the German state.

The great superiority of men and materials possessed by the alliance of the UK, France and Tsarist Russia over Germany and Austria gave rise to the expectation that the war would be over by Christmas. In the event, Germany, knowing it was fighting for its life, resisted these superior forces for more than four years. But in the end Germany was destroyed. And for good measure the United Kingdom declared war on the Ottoman Empire in November 1914, and destroyed that too.

The Great War cost something in the region of ten million lives. Three great states were destroyed in the course of it and a fourth collapsed.

Although the Home Rule Party had been elected to gain self-government in Ireland, it threw all its energies into this war to destroy the German, Austrian and Turkish states and to extend the British Empire. Redmond became the operator of a transmission belt conveying Irish cannon-fodder to Flanders and Mesopotamia. The operation went smoothly for a year and three-quarters. It was then disrupted by a military insurrection in Ireland.

A minority within the nationalist movement had in 1914 dissented from the alliance of Home Rule Ireland with Imperialist Britain. Some of these were merely nationalist in outlook, and made no effort to assess the war as an international event. England's difficulty was Ireland's opportunity, and that was enough. But two of the most effective leaders of the dissent did assess the war in its international context and their judgment of it led them to commit themselves on the German side. Their conclusions are well summed up in the titles of their main articles on the issue: Roger Casement's **The Crime Against Europe** and James Connolly's **The War Upon The German Nation**. And their alliance with Germany was ratified in the 1916 Proclamation by the reference to "gallant allies in Europe".

Casement went to Germany and tried to recruit an Irish Brigade amongst Irish prisoners-of-war for service against Britain. But the cannon-fodder recruited by Redmond proved to be utterly loyal to the British Empire.

Connolly had salvaged a small army from the 1913 Dublin strike. He determined to make war on Britain with this army. And his newspaper, The Workers' Republic, leaves no room for doubt that he saw an Irish blow against Britain, while Britain was engaged in its work of destroying Germany, as being international and socialist by virtue of the German connection.

The shock of the Easter Rising diminished the effectiveness of Redmondite recruiting. It made people stop and think. The blind allegiance of nationalist Ireland to Imperialist Britain decayed. An alternative centre of state formation, unconnected with British parties or the Westminster Parliament, was formed in Ireland. It resulted in the establishment of an actual Irish state within three years of the Rising. Having destroyed Germany, Britain made war on the new Irish state for two years before making terms with it.

Nationalist Ireland was thoroughly enmeshed in British affairs in 1914. The unquestioning and unquestioned allegiance of the Home Rule Party and most of the people to Britain in its war on Germany, Austria and Turkey is sufficient proof of that. Five years later Ireland was living its own separate political life outside the British framework, and six years later it was at war with Britain.

The condition of things actually existing in 1921 was scarcely imaginable in 1914. And it was scarcely possible in 1921 to remember the actually existing condition of things as it was in 1914.

In 1914 Ireland was in process of being integrated with Britain under the form of Home Rule and under the hegemony of Liberal Imperialism. The Ulster Unionist resistance was delaying the conclusion of that process, but the delay had the effect of deepening the connection between nationalist Ireland and Liberal Imperialist Britain.

The conflict of Unionism and Nationalism in Ireland became the central conflict of United Kingdom politics in 1912. The Home Rule conflict of 1912-14 was not a conflict between Ireland and Britain. It was a conflict within the mainstream politics of the UK state.

In the 1640s an English civil war tore Ireland apart. Between 1912 and 1914 the conflict of Irish Catholic-nationalist and Ulster Unionist threatened to tear England apart.

The Anglophile German ambassador in London, Prince Lichnowsky, who understood that the apparent ferocity of party conflict in England was superficial froth overlaying a basic consensus, was astonished to find in 1913-14 that party antagonism had become real, i.e. that it had been carried over into social and private life:

"The Englishman is either in society or wishes to get into society. It is his constant effort to be a man of distinction, a gentleman; and even men of modest origin, such as Mr. Asquith, wish to move in society and prefer to meet handsome and fashionable women.

"The British gentleman, no matter to which party he belongs, enjoys the same education, goes to the same colleges and universities, engages in the same sports... They have all played cricket and football in their youth; they have the same habits of life, and spend the week-end in the country. The division between the parties is not social. It is purely political. But in the last few years it has developed into a social cleavage, insofar as the politicians of the two camps avoid social contact with each other. The two camps could not be brought together even on the neutral territory of an embassy, because, since the Home Rule and Veto Bills, the Unionists have put the Radicals under a ban. When the King and Queen dined with us a few months after my arrival, Lord Londonderry left the house after dinner so as not to remain in the company of Sir Edward Grey." (**My London Mission**. The Veto Bill gave

6

the Commons the power to proceed with legislation after a certain term without the agreement of the Lords.)

Party rivalry had ceased to be a game. It had become a conflict in dead earnest and was threatening to rupture the state. And no settlement was in prospect in July 1914 when an opportunity to make war on Germany suddenly presented itself.

Although the Home Rule conflict had its source in a basic incompatibility of culture and temperament between the old Ulster Protestant community and the new Catholic-nationalist development in Ireland, it did not develop as a localised antagonism of those communities. It was assimilated into the main party-political divisions in the state, and by the summer of 1914 it was threatening to tear the state apart.

(The leading writer on the British Constitution, A.V. Dicey, a Liberal Unionist, who expounded the doctrine of Parliamentary sovereignty with great force and clarity, declared as follows: "If the Government, without any dissolution of Parliament, avail themselves of the Parliament Act to transform the Home Rule Bill into the Home Rule Act, 1914, it will be in form   a law but will lack all constitutional authority, and the duty of Unionists will be to treat it as a measure which lacks the sanction of the nation" (**A Fool's Paradise** Being A Constitutionalist's Criticism On The Home Rule Bill Of 1912. 1913, p117). And further: "What are the limits within which the tyranny either of a king or of a democracy justifies civil war is not an inquiry into which I will enter" (p127).

Dicey's **Law Of The Constitution**, first published in 1885, is still in print today as one of the major works on its subject. In an Introduction to the 8th edition (1915) he included the following reflections, prompted by the Parliament Act and the Home Rule Bill: "a real limit to the exercise of sovereignty is imposed not by the laws of man but by the nature of things" (pxxvi); the influence of law had been weakened "by the misdevelopment of party government" (pxlii); "No sensible man can refuse to admit that crises occasionally, though very rarely, arise when armed rebellion against unjust and oppressive laws may be morally justifiable" (pxliii); "The Parliament Act enables of majority of the House of Commons to resist or overrule the will of the electors or, in other words, of the nation" (pliii).

When the Liberal Party in power took up the Home Rule issue and pressed it to the brink of civil war against the Tory/Liberal Unionist combination (the Unionist Party), the Home Rule Party became entirely dependent on it. The Home Rule issue ceased to be a source of division between Ireland (or three-quarters of it) and England when it became the central issue of British politics. And as the Home Rule issue was assimilated into the party politics of the state, the Home Rule Party became an adjunct of the Liberal Party in substance while retaining its separate form.

In a great many instances the relationship of Home Rulers to the Liberal Party went beyond dependence and became enthusiastic advocacy. Fiery nationalist journalists became fiery radical journalists in the Liberal press. And it seems to me that they played an important part in getting British war propaganda off to a good (or bad) start during the first week or two of the war while many of the less adaptable English Liberal journalists were still hesitant. Whatever debt the Redmondites owed to the Liberals was paid back with interest in August 1914.

The consequences in Ireland of this intimacy between Redmondism and the governing party in the state were wholly damaging. The Redmondites relied on the brute power of the British state to establish them in office as the Home Rule Government of all Ireland. Confident of that power, they felt that all they need do about the Ulster Unionists was insult them. Therefore, when the power-play failed and Irish affairs were displaced from the centre of British politics, the antagonism within Ireland was deeper than ever before.

Canon Sheehan, the inspirer of the All-for-Ireland League, and William O'Brien, its leader, who stirred up the county of Cork against Redmondism and caused it to lose all but one of its Parliamentary seats there in the 1910 General Elections, alleged that the Home Rule Party had become a virtual sub-committee of the Liberal Party. When I first came across that allegation I assumed that it was a considerable exaggeration, justifiable in the heat of political conflict but not really true. But the more I got to know about those years the less I felt that there was any exaggeration at all in that view.

Sheehan and O'Brien, who were in earnest about fostering independent national life in Ireland, saw that the policy of relying on British power to establish the framework of an all-Ireland state was self-contradictory, and that its visible results were a sapping of the internal vigour of the Home Rule movement as a national movement and an intensifying stubbornness on the part of the Ulster Protestants. Their view was that the Irish national movement could only make itself fit to govern all Ireland by ceasing to be Catholic-nationalist and by dealing with the Ulster Protestants directly rather than through the intermediacy of the British state. Unfortunately, although Redmondism broke down under the stresses of the war of destruction against Germany to which it committed nationalist Ireland, the Redmondite attitude to the Ulster Protestant community has been carried over into all varieties of contemporary nationalist politics.

The convergence of the Home Rule Party and the Liberal Party occurred at a moment when the Liberal Party was itself undergoing a drastic change of character. The Liberal leadership had fallen into the hands of the Liberal Imperialist group, with Asquith as Prime Minister, Haldane as Minister for War and Grey as Foreign Minister. These three, along with Churchill who had become a Liberal because of dissatisfaction with the more modest imperialist ambition of the Tories, exercised a tight control over foreign policy and over war and peace. It was they who decided in late July, 1914, to avail of the Balkan crisis as an opportunity to make war on Germany. And they manipulated events in late July and early August so as to bring the bulk of the Liberal Party into line with their object.

The Liberal Imperialist tendency was fostered by Lord Roseberry in the 1890s. It took definite factional shape during the Boer War. Adherents of the older Liberalism disapproved of that war. A trio of ambitious young Liberals, (Asquith, Haldane and Grey, all barristers), supported the war both in principle and with regard to its conduct by terrorist methods applied against the civil population— scorched earth and concentration camps.

For a number of years the Liberal Party was in effect two parties locked in bitter conflict. That conflict was never formally resolved. The Liberal Imperialists never won a formal victory within the party. A *modus vivendi* between the two was established which enabled the party to win the 1906 election under the leadership of Campbell-Bannermann, who had opposed the Boer War. But Campbell-Bannermann gave the Liberal Imperialists the offices they were chiefly interested in. Of particular consequence was his appointment of Haldane to the War Office and Grey to the Foreign Office.

When Campbell-Bannermann retired with a fatal illness in 1908 he was succeeded as Prime Minister by Asquith. Haldane and Grey continued their preparations for a war on Germany. And a few years later Churchill was put in command of the Navy. But a majority of the Liberal MPs remained strongly attached to the sentiments of the older Liberalism and they needed skilful handling in July/August 1914 to develop them into warmongers.

T.P. O'Connor, a leading Home Rule politician and journalist of Parnellite origin, published a biography of Campbell-Bannermann in 1907. The Home Rulers were at that point still firmly aligned with the Gladstonian Liberals against the Imperialists.

In 1917 O'Connor contributed a chapter on The Irish In Great Britain to a book of war propaganda entitled **Irish Heroes In The War**. This book was about the raising of the Tyneside Irish Brigade and the honours won by it. In August 1914 Joseph Cowen, a Liberal notable in Tyneside, put up £10,000 to equip three Newcastle battalions, one of which was to be Irish. O'Connor remarks that Cowen was "like his father, at once democratic and Imperialist." (p28.)

In 1915 O'Connor made a propaganda tour of the United States. "He was officially thanked by Lord Grey of Fallodon, then Foreign Secretary, for his 'excellent work in placing the cause of the Allies before American public opinion'." (**T.P. O'Connor** by Hamilton Fyfe, 1930, p238.)

"Then there was in December 1913 the dinner offered to T.P.... on the occasion of the rebirth of his Weekly, a gathering composed almost entirely of men distinguished either in politics or journalism. Lord Curzon as Chairman described the guest as 'one of the most remarkable men and one of the most faithful friends they had ever met...' Speeches equally warm were made by Winston Churchill, Lord Derby, the American Ambassador (Mr. Harvey), and T.P.s old enemy, Lord Carson." (ibid. p304.)

Because the actual history of Ireland from about 1900 to 1916 has not been written, it is taken as self evident that Irish nationalism and British Imperialism were contraries. As bare concepts they may be contraries. But as actual movements they converged in the course of the Home Rule conflict. It required no maverick behaviour, no eccentric individualism, to carry T.P. O'Connor to a dinner given in his honour by Curzon, Churchill and Carson.

Erskine Childers

Most of the Home Rulers became Imperialists under the influence of the Home Rule crisis of 1912-14, when the Liberal Imperialists in power acted more purposefully on their behalf than the Gladstonian Liberals had ever done. But some had been Liberal Imperialists all along. Chief among these was Erskine Childers.

Childers ran guns into Howth harbour in late July 1914, a week before going off to make war on Germany. Sixteen years earlier, when he was a Clerk in the House of Commons, he had volunteered for service against the Boers in an upper middle class artillery unit. On his return from South Africa he wrote a volume of The Times history of the war—the volume dealing with the guerrilla phase—in which he justified the concentration camps in principle while conceding that in practice they had not been as effective militarily as had been hoped.

The following passage is interesting on a number of counts. Britain's war propaganda in the Great War suggested that Casement had done something particularly evil and unusual when he tried to recruit an Irish Brigade in the German prisoner-of-war camps to fight against Britain. Yet Childers here describes how Britain put pressure on captured Boers to fight against their own people. He also demonstrates that the Liberal Imperialist was just as racist as the Boer, and with less excuse:

"The army was now (May 1901) deriving much informal assistance from two alien sources, Boer and native. Surrendered Boers had for some time past been taking an active part in assisting British operations. Several hundred 'Burgh Police' as they were called, were associated with the South African Constabulary in maintaining protected area round Bloemfontein... But it was in the capacity of scouts and spies that the burghers were most useful. It must be borne in mind that defection had not yet assumed any formal or recognised character. The influential men among those who had surrendered in the winter of 1900, and had taken the oath of allegiance—men such as Piet de Wet... and General Andries... still held aloof from any active participation in the war. For the present (apart from the Bloemfontein burghers) defection merely represented leakage from the lower class of Boers, *bywoners* or landless men, who had no stake in the country and held the ties of commando very lightly.

"Increasing use was made of the native population for miscellaneous purposes directly or indirectly connected with the war. As transport-drivers, cattle-guards, labourers and so on,unarmed natives had for long been employed, and continued to be employed, in large numbers. It was now becoming the practice to arm natives for directly military purposes. In all cases the original motive was that of supplying means of self-defence against an enemy who attached very little value to the life of a Kaffir. On broad grounds of policy nobody will deny that, in a war between two white races, destined in the future to live side by side in the midst of a vast coloured population, natives should be armed only in case of the last necessity. This necessity can be clearly shown in the case of the predominately native districts of Cape Colony... where one or two causeless barbarities were perpetrated by the Boers. In the north-eastern districts, where the white population was very sparse, half-caste Bastards and Cape Boys were enrolled in considerable numbers for local defence... The Zululand Police were most loyal and useful... We do not intend to argue the question at length... The only justification was sheer military necessity, and this was the answer given to the protests of the Boer leaders. It is hard, in view of the immense difficulties which faced the British in South Africa, to pass unreserved condemnation upon the practice; but it is necessary to insist that a nation which is compelled to draw upon such sources to supply its military needs incurs risks which are none the less real because they are not immediately apparent.

"Although the Boer view of the natives was different from, and repugnant to, the traditionally humane British view, it did recognise the necessity of maintaining white prestige...

"Meanwhile in a civil sense, the vast battle-ground was being slowly depopulated, the ring cleared, so to speak, for the two combatants, by the deliberate action of the stronger. Farm after farm was being visited and its non-combatants transported to centres where they were fed and educated by their enemies. In May there were in round numbers 77,000 white persons in the concentration camps and 21,000 coloured people. The figures rose by leaps and bounds during the following months, reaching their highest level, 118,000 and 43,000 respectively, in October. In March the Transvaal and Free State camps had passed from the control of the military administration... to the civil power; but in Natal camps were not transferred until November. The full extent of embarrassment caused by the policy of depopulation was now clearly visible. The burghers had been encouraged to continue their armed resistance, and at the same time, owing to the condition of the camps, were able to make political use in England and Europe of the sufferings of their women and children. In part these complaints were insincere, for it is abundantly clear that they were heartily glad to be relieved of the responsibility for the maintenance of their families, and would not, on any account, have resumed the burden. But in part... the complaints were well grounded. Growing at a rapid rate, without adequate provision for their growth or prudent allowance for the helplessness and ignorance of their occupants, some of the camps, humane as their intention was, had fallen into a far from satisfactory state. The death-rate, especially among children, was terribly harsh... During the early months of 1901 the evil grew without much general recognition, but in June, in consequence of the researches of Miss Emily Hobhouse,... considerable agitation was caused in England. Miss Hobhouse was not altogether politic or temperate in presenting her case; hence a bitter controversy of a semi-political character, in which the true issue was lost under heated polemics concerning British humanity in the war. The truth was that while the concentration system caused far less misery and loss than would have been suffered had the families remained on the veld, the way in which it was carried out was open to much criticism. This eventually was recognised." **(The Times History of the War in South Africa, 1899-1902.** Vol V, Chapter X, "Kitchener And The Guerrilla Army". pp248-253.)

Childers was neither a Liberal nor a Home Ruler when he went off to make war on the Boer Republics. He became a Liberal in the course of that atrocious war in which Britain pioneered the mode of total war—war waged against societies and not merely armies—which set the pattern for warfare in the twentieth century. He did not become a Liberal in revulsion against that war, but in affirmation of it. Then, as a Liberal Imperialist, he became a Home Ruler.

Germany did not make war on Britain while it was preoccupied with its military conquest of the Boer Republics, nor did it give military assistance to the Boers. It only indicated that it thought justice lay with the Boers. But if Germany had been minded to make war on Britain, it might have done so on very favourable terms during the Boer War. And that thought preyed on the mind of Childers and others.

Wellington, while serving his military apprenticeship in India, once conducted a manoeuvre in the presence of the enemy which would have enabled a competent enemy commander to destroy him as he destroyed Marshal Marmont's army at Salamanca many years later. The enemy commander possibly did not realise that he had missed a golden opportunity, but Wellington realised it and determined that he would never again disturb his own peace of mind by presenting such an opportunity. And so it was with Britain with regard to Germany after the Boer War.

The Kaiser, unlike Wellington's foe in India, did not see Britain as the enemy. He did not seize his golden opportunity because he was not aiming to do what it was an opportunity to do. But influential elements within the British ruling class saw the double hypothesis that *if* Germany had been intent on making war on Britain it *might* have done so with advantage during the Boer War, and they determined not to let it happen again. One way to prevent it from happening again was to take Germany at a disadvantage and crush it. And in order to make war on Germany, Germany had to be depicted as an evil power. (In earlier times it might have been sufficient to show that there was a conflict of interest with Germany. But Britain was now a democracy. The Nonconformist Conscience was a power in the land. And the Nonconformist Conscience did not pursue interests, like the normal ruck of humanity. It did battle with evil. Therefore if the Germans were to be made war upon they had to be depicted as a force of evil.)

In 1903 Childers published **The Riddle Of The Sands**, which was the pioneer work of anti-German propaganda on a mass scale. It is as poisonous as anything produced by the hacks of Oxford, Cambridge and Fleet Street after August 4th 1914, but it is so well written that it remains one of the great adventure novels of English literature. It is the story of how an honest Englishman yachting in the North Sea discovers the secret German preparations, supervised by the Kaiser himself, for an invasion of England.

Having presented Germany to the British public at large as an evil and treacherous enemy, Childers then involved himself in the militarism of the Liberal Imperialist era (1906-1914). In 1910 he published a well-argued book (**War And The Arme Blanche**), urging, on the basis of the experience of the Boer War, that the Cavalry should be reformed into mounted infantry.

"My central purpose in this volume is to submit to searching criticism the armament of cavalry. That armament now consists of a rifle and a sword in all regiments, with the addition of a lance in the case of Lancers. I shall argue that the steel weapons ought either to be discarded or denied all influence on tactics, and a pure type of mounted rifleman substituted for the existing hybrid type." (p1.)

"Shock action, consigned to complete oblivion in South Africa and to equally complete oblivion in Manchuria, still holds first place in the training of the Cavalry soldier." (p7.)

"The fine old word 'Cavalry' simply means horse-soldiers without regard to weapon." (p15.)

But this Liberal Imperialist utilitarianism was not welcome in traditional military circles. The attraction of the Cavalry lay in the "shock action"—the impact of charging Cavalry on the line of infantry, breaking it and leading to the rout—and in the ecstasy felt in the pursuit of the broken infantry as cold steel slashed through warm flesh and brains and blood spurted out. Childers might argue a powerful case that this source of pleasure was unlikely to recur in the age of repeating rifles and machine guns, but the fox-hunting class was not prepared to abandon hope under mere force of argument. There was, however, support for the reform at the highest level. War And The Arme Blanche appeared with an introduction by Field-Marshal Earl Roberts. (The term "arme blanche" was taken to be understood by all the readers for whom the book was intended. It is not explained, and I have not been able to find it in any dictionary. But the meaning in context seems clear enough: it is the arm of a Cavalryman wielding cold steel.)

Childers here gives us some further reflections on the Boer War:

"Roberts, as early as September 1900, had enjoined the destruction of crops, and, under certain conditions, of farms, though comparatively little had been accomplished when he quitted the command. Kitchener initiated a plan of systematic devastation, with its corollary, the systematic deportation of non-combatants to concentration camps. With the ethical and political aspects of this measure we are not now concerned. Its military result was to retard the education and restrict the fighting efficiency of our mounted troops by setting before them two incompatible aims: that of grappling with the enemy, and that of destroying his crops and cattle and deporting his families. The latter aim, which was secondary, too often tended to become primary simply because it was the easiest to put into practice, and human nature is prone to follow the line of least resistance.

"Another doubtful precedent, closely allied with the last, and only to be justified as a *pis aller* to meet an immensely difficult case, was the system of "drives"—the system, that is, of sweeping defined tracts of country with large groups of columns, to formal plans worked out in a central staff department and controlled in execution from that department. This, broadly speaking, was Kitchener's method of dealing with the guerrilla war." (p224/5.)

Although the use of Cavalry to herd the population into concentration camps retarded the development of its proper military function, "by a throttling, starving process it eventually brought the Boers to their knees." (p225.)

And here is Childers conclusion about Kitchenette conduct of the war:

"His genius was for organisation; his countrymen profited by that genius, and it ill becomes them to cavil at the defects which were its inevitable accomplishment." (p226.)

Having "brought the Boers to their knees" the Unionist Government did not humiliate them further, as the Lloyd George Government insisted on doing to the Germans in 1919. Childers defends Government policy in the matter:

"We had taken up arms to secure the political equality of our countrymen, and we had already secured that object beyond question, their annexation as well. To go farther, and aim at so cowing the Boer national spirit as to gain a permanent political ascendancy for ourselves was an object beyond our power or will to achieve, and beyond the power or will of any free democracy or confederation of free democracies of the British Imperial type to achieve. Peaceable political fusion under our own flag was the utmost we could secure. That meant a conditional Boer surrender, on a promise of future autonomy. The unconditional surrender which Lord Milner was anxious to obtain, however long and bitter a struggle it entailed, could scarcely have led to peaceable fusion." (p227/8.)

"Did we really in our hearts desire such crushing victories as would shatter the spirit of our opponents and lay the foundation for a racial ascendancy, as opposed to a racial fusion, in South Africa?" (p176.)

Childers does not have the blacks in mind when he refers to "racial fusion". His only concern is with relations between the British and the Boers. And in fact the "racial fusion" was only a superficial show put on by an element of the Boer population under the influence of British conquest.

Britain either did far too little or far too much in South Africa for any good to come of it. Under British rule, mediated by Quislings, the nucleus of Boer society withdrew into itself culturally, elaborated Scriptural injunctions into a comprehensive political system, and ousted Britain's protege, Smuts, in 1948. It is unlikely that the apartheid system put into effect after 1948 would ever have materialised if Britain had let the Boer Republics be.

The manipulation of peoples by stick and carrot proved no more successful when conducted by Britain in South Africa than it did when conducted by Russia in Poland.

But to return to the *arme blanche*:

"Is it not a commonplace in every Englishman's mouth that, hard and bitter as the struggle was, 'no other nation'—and among other nations Germany is often instanced—could have engaged in it so successfully as ourselves? There is sound truth in the boast... And when we envisage a European war, are we to forget this boast and, ignoring not only our own priceless experience, but our innate capacities, revert to the antiquated European system...

"Disguise it as we may, the real peculiarity of the Boer War was that the Boer horsemen did not carry steel weapons. European Cavalries do."

In the event, War And The Arme Blanche was much ado about nothing.

Cavalry played little or no part in the war against Germany. The Germans in retreat devised the system of trenches protected by barbed wire and defended with machine guns, which for four solid years consumed Allied cannon-fodder at the rate of 1,500 every day.

Childers made a further contribution to British military thought with **German Influence On British Cavalry**, which was published in 1911, the same year as his book on **The Framework Of Home Rule**. There was no anti-imperialist rhetoric in his advocacy of Home Rule. His purpose was to include a Home Rule Ireland as a willing participant in the Empire, as he imagined South Africa had become. It was in Ulster that he saw a force disruptive of Empire. He refers to "the almost inexplicable contradiction which has existed for so long between Unionism and Imperialism" (p340).

Here is the gist of his argument:

"If the Sinn Fein alternative meant anything at all, it meant complete separation, which Ireland does not want, and a final abandonment of constitutional methods. If another Home Rule Bill were to fail, Sinn Fein would undoubtedly redouble its strength. Its ideas are sane and sound. They are at bottom exactly the ideas which activate every progressive and spirited community." (p168.)

"As long as Great Britain insists… upon deciding Irish questions by party majorities fluctuating from Toryism to Radicalism, and thereby compels Ireland to send parties to Westminster whose *raison d' etre* is, not to represent crystallised Irish opinion on Irish domestic questions… but to assert or deny the fundamental right of Ireland to settle her own domestic questions, so long will these dislocations continue, to the grave prejudice of Ireland and to the deep discredit of Great Britain.

"Ireland… has no organic national life. Apart from the abstract but paramount question of Home Rule, there are no formed political principles or parties. Such parties as there are have no relation to the economic life of the country, and all interests suffer daily in consequence." (p169/70.)

"In a normal country you would find urban and agricultural interests distinctly represented, but not in Ireland. We should expect to find clear-cut opinions on Tariff Reform and Free Trade. No such opinions exist. On the other hand, agreement on important industrial and agricultural questions finds not the smallest reflection in Parliamentary representation… The Protestant tenant-farmers of Ulster have identical interests with those of the other Provinces… but for the most part… they vote Unionist. The two great towns, Dublin and Belfast, are divided by the most irrational antagonism. Labourers, both rural and urban, have distinct and important interests: the rural labourers have no spokesmen, the town-labourers only one. It was admitted to me by a Unionist organiser in Belfast that that city, but for the Home Rule issue, would probably return four labour members." (p170/71.)

(In fact, rural labour was quite effectively represented in parts of Munster through the Land And Labour movement. But, since Land And Labour joined with William O'Brien's All-For-Ireland League in ousting the Home Rule Party from eight of the nine Cork seats in the 1910 General Elections, Childers naturally took no account of it.)

"The purpose of the Irish Unionist Party in the Commons is purely negative, to defeat Home Rule. It does not represent North East Ulster or any other fragment of Ireland, in any sense but that. It is passionately sentimental and absolutely unrepresentative of the practical, virile genius of Ulster industry." (p182.)

" 'Loyalty' to the Crown is a false issue. Disloyalty to the Crown is a negligible factor in all parts of Ireland. Loyalty or disloyalty to a certain political system is the real matter at issue.

"At the present day the really serious objection to Home Rule on the part of the leading Ulster Unionists seems to be economic. They have built up thriving trades under the Union. They have the closest business connections with Great Britain, and a mutual fabric of credit. They cherish sincere and profound apprehensions that their business prosperity will suffer by the change in the form of government. To scoff at these apprehensions is absurd and impolitic in the last degree. But to reason against them is also almost a fruitless labour. Those who feel them vaguely picture an Irish Parliament composed of Home Rulers and Unionists, in the same proportion to the population as at present, and divided by the same bitter and demoralising feuds. But there will be no Home Rulers after Home Rule, that is to say, if the Home Rule conceded is sufficient. I believe that Ulster Unionists do not realise either the beneficent transformation which will follow a change from sentimental to practical politics in Ireland—or the enormous weight which their own fine qualities and strong economic position will give them in the settlement of the Irish question." (p185.)

"What is best for Ireland will be best for the Empire... If it were for Ireland's moral and material good to become an independent nation, it would be Great Britain's interest to encourage her to secede and assume the position of a small state like Belgium, whose independence in our own interests we guarantee. Since nobody of sense, in or out of Ireland, supposes that her interest lies in that direction, we need not consider the point." (p189)

"Home Rule will eventually come. Within the Empire, the utmost achieved by the government of white men without their own consent is to weaken their capacity to assume the sacred responsibility of self-government. It is impossible to kill the idea of Home Rule, though it is possible, by retarding its realization, to pervert some of its strength and beauty, and to diminish the vital energy on which its fruition depends." (p339.)

"The Empire owes everything to those who have disputed, sometimes at the cost of their lives, illegitimate authority. Some day the politicians who now spend sleepless nights...in ransacking the ancient files of the world's Press for proofs that Mr. Redmond once used words signifying that he aimed at 'separation'—whatever that phrase may mean—will regret that they ever demeaned themselves by such petty labour, and will place Mr. Redmond among the number of those who have saved the Empire from the consequences of its own errors." (p341.)

Such was the Liberal Imperialist scheme for Ireland. Being myself the product of a community which had already in 1910 overthrown Redmondism electorally and embarked on a different line of social and political development, I cannot regret that things did not turn out as Childers hoped. But when one views the matter more objectively the question that arises is: Why did the Liberal Imperialist scheme not work out? It seemed to have almost everything going for it in 1912.

The argument that it failed because a million Ulster Unionists were insufficiently Imperialist and excessively "sentimental" won't do. The Unionist resistance of 1912-14 and the determination shown by the Government gave a subjective force to the Imperialist connection within nationalist Ireland that had not been there before 1912. Ten years earlier the Home Rule movement had been anti-Imperialist in general sentiment, and its alliance with the Liberal Party had been a matter of expediency. But by 1914 the Liberal connection had become a genuine attachment; and, due to the fundamental change in Liberal philosophy, it had become an Imperialist connection.

The secret arming of the Ulster Volunteers in March 1914 led to the arming of the Irish Volunteers in July. If the arming of the Irish Volunteers had been done by the Fenians, then it might be said that the Ulster resistance had derailed the scheme of Imperial Home Rule. But it was not done by the Fenians. It was done by a group of Anglo-Irish gentlemen and ladies: the Childerses, the Spring Rices, Alice Stopford Green, Lord Ashbourne, Captain George FitzHardinge Berkley, Sir Alexander Lawrence, Darrell Figgis, Conor O'Brien, Hugh Vere O'Brien, Capt. Gordon Shephard, James Creed Meredith, Lady Alice Young, Sir Thomas Myles, Hervey de Montmorency and Roger Casement.

There is a good account of the affair by F. X. Martin O.S.A., in **The Howth Gun Running**, Browne and Nolan, 1964. Martin says in summary:

> "A survey of the group who organized the gun-running reveals that on the whole they were Anglo-Irish, Liberal, Protestant Home Rulers, and of the upper and professional classes. Their mutual bonds were as much social and personal as political. In many ways the gun-running had a family air about it." (pXIX.)

The guns were landed from two yachts. On July 26 Childers, with his yacht *Asgard*, landed his consignment at Howth Harbour in broad daylight. Part of that consignment was carried into Dublin in an exhibitionist manner, observed by the police and the Army, and leading at the end of the day to the shooting by the King's Own Scottish Borderers at Bachelors Walk in which three civilians were killed. (The officer in command was reprimanded soon afterwards following an inquiry.)

On August 1st Sir Thomas Myles, with his yacht *Chotah* landed his consignment more discreetly at Kilcool under cover of darkness. The *Chotah* guns had been taken on board at sea from Conor O'Brien's yacht, *Kelpie*. Immediately after the gun-running Childers and O'Brien went on active service with the British Navy for the war on Germany. Myles became a Lieutenant Colonel in the British Army (in the medical service) but he does not seem to have been posted to France.

The gun-running did not subvert the Imperial framework of Home Rule, but confirmed it. And the nationalist Irish response to the war seemed to clinch it. But then over the next few years everything went wrong. Irish Home Rule did not survive the War. But the failure of Irish Home Rule was one of the very least disasters, if a disaster at all, in the great universal catastrophe for which Liberal Imperialism was responsible.

Liberal Unionism And Liberal Imperialism.

British political life, which is usually represented as being firmly based on empirical foundations, was actually in a highly volatile ideological condition during the quarter century leading up to 1914. The Liberal Party was the most volatile and ideological part of it. And the Irish Home Rule movement became identified with the most unstable element of Liberalism: Liberal Imperialism.

Liberalism divided into three tendencies: Liberal Unionism, Liberal Imperialism, with Gladstonian Liberalism (for which "old-fashioned Liberalism" might be a better name) as an indefinite and evaporating quantity between them.

In 1886 the Liberal Party split over Gladstone's first Home Rule Bill. The more vigorous, radical, and socially concerned wing of the Party, led by Joseph Chamberlain, opposed Home Rule. They left the party and, as Liberal Unionists, joined the Tories in a new body called the Unionist Party. Ulster Unionism, which since 1921 is what has been designated by the name, "the Unionist Party", was a minor element in the Unionist Party of 1886 to 1914.

That Unionist Party governed for most of the period between 1886 and 1906. It was Imperialist and social reformist. Its Irish administration provided the most thorough reforming government Ireland has ever had, enacting both local government democracy and the 1903 land reform.

The Liberal residue led by Gladstone remained a Home Rule, laissez-faire, anti-Imperialist Party as long as Gladstone lived. (It was anti-Imperialist in a sense peculiar to the period: it was not in favour of expanding the Empire.) Gladstone died in 1898. The Boer War was launched by the Unionist Government in 1899. The ambitious younger element in the Liberal Party, led by Asquith, Haldane and Grey, availed of the Chauvinist spirit generated by the War to get on the Imperialist bandwagon.

The Liberal Imperialists not only followed the Liberal Unionists on the issues of Imperialism and social reform, but outstripped them. (Those two issues were then seen as being interconnected.) But they retained Gladstone's Home Rule policy, intending that Home Rule Ireland should form part of an Imperial structure.

The war against the Boer Republics fell into two phases: the war of territorial conquest (1899/1900) and the suppression of the guerrilla resistance (1900/1902). The chief Government propagandist in the War was Arthur Conan Doyle, the inventor of Sherlock Holmes. Doyle was a Liberal Unionist. He published two books on the War. The first, **The Great Boer War**, is dated September 1900, and is written as if the War had ended. The second, **The War In South Africa: Its Causes and Conduct** was published in 1902 in English, French, German and half a dozen other European languages. It is a justification of the measures by which the guerrilla resistance was suppressed, and was distributed around the world by the Foreign Office.

Doyle's task in the first book was to show why it was morally right for Britain to act in breach of its Treaty recognition of the Boer Republics.

In the early 19th century Britain had, by conquest and purchase, acquired the Dutch possessions on the southern coast of Africa. Many of the Boer farmers, wanting to live according to their own fashion, trekked into the interior and established Republics which Britain recognised. Britain had now embarked on a war of conquest against those Republics. How could that be justified?

Doyle argued thus:

"The title deeds to the estate are... good, but there is one flaw, one singular and ominous flaw in their provisions. The ocean has marked three boundaries to it, but the fourth is undefined. There is no word of the 'Hinterland', for neither the term nor the idea had then been thought of. Had Great Britain bought those vast regions which extended beyond the settlements. Or were the discontented Dutch at liberty to pass onward and found fresh nations to bar the path of the Anglo-Celtic colonists? In this question lay the germ of all the trouble to come. An American would realise the point at issue if he could conceive that after the founding of the United States the Dutch inhabitants of the State of New York had trekked to the westward and established fresh communities under a new flag. Then, when the American population overtook these western States, they would be face to face with the problem which this country has had to solve. If they found these new States fiercely anti-American and extremely unprogressive they would experience that aggravation of their difficulties with which our statesmen have had to deal." (The Great Boer War. 1900. Chapter I.)

The Boer Republics lay across the British path to Central Africa where gold and diamonds and valuable raw materials and space for the expanding "Anglo-

Celtic" race lay. Progress was therefore obstructed. And of course no Treaty, no scrap of paper, can be allowed to stand in the way of progress.

Fourteen years later Germany, caught between the superior force of Russia and France, pleaded military necessity in defence of its violation of Belgian neutrality. British statesmen and intellectuals declared that any nation which pleaded such a defence for the violation of a Treaty must be tainted to the core. These were in great part the very same people who justified the Boer War on the ground of mere imperial ambition and racial expansion and "progress" (which meant British interest).

Doyle's analogy between the Western expansion of the United States and the Northern expansion of British South Africa is no casual comparison. The new Imperialism of the late 19th century was set in the concept of "Greater Britain".

Greater Britain was the vision of J. R. Seeley. Seeley was appointed to the Chair of Modern History at Cambridge through Gladstone's influence in 1869. He was already famous then for a biography of Jesus called **Ecce Homo**. In 1881/2 he delivered two series of lectures at Cambridge which were a watershed in British Imperial thinking. They were published in book form under the title **The Expansion Of England**, but the book was really a pamphlet. All the literary productions which have had a particular and enduring effect on the course of English history have been pamphlets—from Milton, through Halifax, Burnet and Locke, to Burke, Paine, and Carlyle. Academic life in Britain today is such that, even though it is largely Marxist in form, it is inconceivable that it should have any definite and purposeful effect on the conduct of politics. But Seeley's lectures had a very considerable effect. They were not only the last academic product which influence affairs of state: they were the last great pamphlet of English political life—at least I can think of nothing comparable since then. (Joe Keenan suggests the Keynes' **Economic Consequences Of The Peace** is comparable to some extent.)

Seeley's object was to dispel...

"...those vague flourishes which the old school of historians, who according to my view lost themselves in mere narrative, used to add for forms sake before winding up. These vague flourishes usually consisted in some reference to what was called the advance of civilisation." (Lecture 1. Tendency In English History.)

Under the influence of those vague flourishes people supposed that the meaning of English history was an evolution towards Liberty or Democracy, "words which want a great deal of defining". But the democratic movement was a very recent innovation in the affairs of the English State, which had been developing steadily for many centuries. Seeley argued that the long-term meaning of the development of the English State was not some vague abstraction which might be called Liberty, but was the expansion of the English State:

"If we stand aloof a little and follow with our eyes the progress of the English State, the great governed society of English people, in recent centuries, we shall be struck much more by another change [i.e., other than the democratic movement, B.C.], though it has always been less discussed, partly because it proceeded more gradually, partly because it excited less opposition. I mean the simple obvious fact of the English extension of the English name into other countries of the globe, the foundation of greater Britain."

Although India was the oldest and largest part of the Empire, the most significant part was the new colonial development:

"This enormous Indian population does not make part of Greater Britain in the same sense as those ten millions of Englishmen who live outside of the British islands. The latter are of our own blood...The former are of alien race and religion, and are bound to us only by the tie of conquest. It may be fairly questioned whether the possession of India does or ever can increase our power or security... Our colonial Empire stands on quite a different footing; it has some of the fundamental conditions of stability...

"Ten millions of Englishmen beyond the sea... this is something; but it is absolutely nothing compared with what will ultimately, nay with what will speedily, be seen."

Seeley became a Liberal Unionist, but his vision was I think shared by both Liberal Imperialists and Liberal Unionists. He was greatly admired by Cecil Rhodes, who prepared the ground for the Boer War and the British drive towards Central Africa.

Rhodes supported Home Rule on principle as a means of organising the Empire—or the white parts of it—into a coherent Imperial Federation. He contributed £10,000 to Parnell's party in 1888. In 1891 he made a secret contribution of £5,000 to the Liberal Party on condition that a flaw in the First Home Rule Bill (discontinuation of Irish representation in the Imperial Parliament) should be remedied in the Second Home Rule Bill which was then in prospect. The 1892 Bill provided for continuing Irish representation at Westminster, on a reduced scale, after a Dublin Parliament was set up.

The aspirations of the Liberal Unionists, who conducted the war against the Boer Republics, were much more limited, definite and realistic than the aspirations of the Liberal tendency which became Imperialist in the course of the war. As soon as the conquest of the Boer Republics was completed, Joseph Chamberlain proposed that the Empire be consolidated by means of an Imperial Tariff and a Council of the Empire. The Tariff proposal (meaning the development of the Empire as a free trade area protected by tariff) caused considerable discussion within the Unionist Party, where the doctrine of universal free trade had taken deep root. Balfour, the party leader, tried to muffle the issue in the interest of party unity. But Chamberlain resigned from the Cabinet in 1903 in order to be able to advocate tariff reform in the country. (Conan Doyle stood for Parliament in Edinburgh in 1906 as a Liberal Unionist Tariff Reformer.)

The dispute over an Imperial Tariff amongst Unionists was as bitter as the dispute over Imperialism was amongst the Liberals. Seeing the possibility of electoral victory the Liberals (who all remained committed to the doctrine of universal free trade) covered over their own dispute and exploited the Unionist divisions. (Winston Churchill, an ultra-Imperialist Tory member of the Unionist Party went over to the Liberals on the free trade issue.)

British foreign policy counts for little today. Prior to 1914 it counted for as much as American foreign policy does today. The Liberal Government of 1906-15 was essentially unstable in the sphere of foreign policy. In 1906/8, under the nominal Gladstonian leadership of Campbell-Bannerman, the Liberal Imperialists, Grey and Haldane, ran the Foreign and War Offices. And even though the Liberal Imperialist, Asquith, became Prime Minister in 1908, the Parliamentary party remained strongly Gladstonian until August 1914. The Asquith coterie in power conducted a secret foreign policy which was fundamentally at variance with the kind of foreign policy wished for by the bulk of the Liberal Party in the country and in Parliament.

Mr. John Hume used a curious phrase in the Commons debate on the Anglo-Irish Agreement in 1985. He berated the Ulster Unionists for refusing to act in accordance with "the sovereign wish of Parliament". It might be said that in 1906/

14 the Government refused to act in accordance with the sovereign wish of Parliament. But the sovereign wish of Parliament is diffuse and insubstantial, especially with regard to foreign affairs, such as relations with Germany or the governing of Northern Ireland. There was evidence in plenty prior to August 1914 of what the Government was up to in the world. Roger Casement read the signs if the Gladstonian Liberal MPs did not. From which it seems sensible to conclude that in 1906/14 Gladstonian Liberalism was living beyond its time, and should be regarded as a form of nostalgia rather than as a form of politics.

The effective choice was between the foreign policy of Liberal Unionism and the foreign policy of Liberal Imperialism.

The foreign policy advocated by Joseph Chamberlain, corresponding to his Imperial tariff and Council of the Empire, was alliance with Germany and the United States. The implication of his combined home (and colonial) and foreign policies was that the Empire should be consolidated and the framework of world affairs stabilised by an alliance of the three major progressive states, which would curb the expansionism of the major authoritarian state, Tsarist Russia.

The foreign policy of the Liberal Imperialists was unlimited expansion of British Imperial power on the basis of universal free trade, and alliance with Tsarist Russia against Germany. There could be no world stability while the most powerful state in the world operated such a policy. And if it had been carried through successfully—if Germany had been destroyed before 1917—the great expansion of Russian power in Europe which happened in the form of Bolshevism in 1945 would have happened in the form of Tsarism in 1915 or 1916.

The Modern Rome.

How did the English state get into this condition?

Anybody who is familiar with what I have written over the years will understand that I did not begin with a prejudice against England. I was as free from that kind of bias as Charles James O'Donnell, who served the British Empire diligently for thirty years before reluctantly concluding that it had gone astray. Not that I have ever been of service to the Empire. Although I was described as an Orange Imperialist in the Dublin press in the early seventies for publishing such pamphlets as **The Economics Of Partition** and **The Two Irish Nations**, I have only ever once spoken to an Orangeman, and my ongoing relationship with the apparatus of the British state has consisted of having my mail opened by it for twenty years, being beaten up by it a few times, and being subject to an ambitious (over-ambitious) attempt at psychological terrorism (which I mention in the pamphlet **Government Without Opposition**, Athol Books, 1986). Having written as I did despite all of that is I think sufficient evidence that I have been entirely dispassionate in my relationship with this former Empire.

I lived until the age of 21 in North West Cork, in a region known as Slieve Luacra, where Gaelic Ireland had its last fling in the 18th century; where landlords were subjected to vigorous terrorist pressure by tenant farmers in the 19th century, and big farmers were taught to respect labour around the turn of the century; where Redmondism was overthrown in 1910; and where the War of Independence was fought intensively in 1920/21. In short, I grew up in a very successful and self-satisfied culture which had won all its wars and had no chip on its shoulder, and I was neither West British nor anti-British.

In London, around 1960, I lived in Camden Town, which was then working class and Irish, and I happened to notice a building called The Working Men's College. I joined it out of curiosity. It was a kind of evening university, founded by the Christian Socialists of the mid-19th century with the object of diverting the workers from Chartism and incorporating them into liberal humanist culture. The Liberal Unionists and Liberal Imperialists, who took a close interest in the political education of the working classes, had been active in it in the period I am discussing here, and so I became familiar with names that were immensely influential in their time, but had been virtually forgotten in English society at large: Frederick Harrisson, Dicey, Haldane, etc.

It so happened that a dozen or so others of a similar disposition to myself, mostly Irish, went to the Working Men's College at the same time to see what it was like. We made it interesting for each other and went there a couple of times a week for a couple of years. And we decided to put its pretensions to the test.

It was conducted supposedly on the lines of Parliamentary government, with a governing Council elected by all members of the College, and an Executive elected by the Council. Myself and Pat Murphy were put up for election to the Council and were elected, and the Council then elected me onto the Executive, and Murphy onto the Finance Committee. The Executive consisted of City millionaires and their retainers and a Scotsman on the make. I had been put on the Executive for the purpose of being tamed. We were representatives of the Camden Town Irish—the first there had ever been, it seemed.

The College had been established to inveigle such as us into British liberal culture, but it was badly out of practice because the likes of us had always kept away from it. The millionaires set out to demonstrate to us that, even though we thought we had something distinctive to say, in fact we hadn't.

To this end, they allowed Murphy to have funding for a magazine to be run independently of the official College magazine, assuming that it would soon run out of steam. I was surprised at the crudity and obviousness of their approach, and determined to ensure that it did not run out of steam. During the following year the dissident magazine established a clear supremacy over the official magazine. And more Camden Town Irish and other working class elements came to the College. The millionaires then panicked and conducted a purge. About twenty people were expelled. The Cromwell of the affair was called Saklatvala, a member of the Tata family, which owned a multinational industrial company. He sent me a letter informing me that I was excluded from the College premises for brawling. The time and place of the alleged brawl were mentioned. I got written statements from everyone who was present in that place at that time contradicting the allegation. But I decided to abide by Saklatvala's Executive action until the next meeting of the Council. On the Parliamentary analogy the one thing that the Executive was certainly *not* entitled to do was deprive an elected Council member of his seat.

I turned up for the next Council meeting just as it was starting. The Chairman (I think he was called the President) was an elderly gentleman called Maurice. He was a descendant of F.D. Maurice, the Christian Socialist who had founded the College, and of General Maurice, who had played a part in subverting the British Empire in the Great War. I had corresponded with him on the principle of the matter beforehand, pointing out that this was the moment of truth for him and his kind as far as the Working Men's College was concerned. (His side of the correspondence was on the notepaper of The Athenaeum Club.)

The Cromwellians had decided on their course of action. As soon as I entered the Parliamentary chamber, Maurice immediately suspended the sitting and called for the police to eject me. The retainers (some of whom I knew to have been batmen in the Army) sat on their hands. When the police came, I explained to them that the College was run on Parliamentary lines, that the Prime Minister had no constitutional authority to deprive me of my seat, that if the Parliament were allowed to debate the issue, and supported a motion by the Prime Minister to expel me, I would go, but as things were I would not go. The police said this was all nonsense—which of course it was—and that Maurice was the Principal and had absolute authority in the matter. I said in that case it was up to to them to remove me. So they picked me up and took me out through lines of my constituents who were shouting "Fascists". I understand that the Working Men's College gave up its political pretensions soon afterwards and became a cramming college for examinations.

This was a trivial incident. But it was my insight into the nature of the English ruling class. Insofar as there was still on English ruling class, Maurice and his colleagues were quite senior members of it. And yet I, an unskilled labourer out of the depths of rural Ireland, got the better of them in the game they chose to play with me. The implication seemed to be that English political culture, which had been dominant in the world only a couple of generations earlier, had become brittle and fraudulent. I did not rush into any far-reaching conclusions on the basis of that experience. I became intrigued by the history of the class of which those people seemed to be a fair sample. Over a period of twenty years I accumulated information about that class and about the Great War. Then I reached the definite conclusion that the English ruling class lost its bearings in the world in the Asquith /Haldane generation. Associated with this was the philosophically complex conclusion that the wrong side had won the Great War. It then followed that whatever might be the other merits of the Easter Rising, it had the very clear and substantial merit of subverting Irish nationalist participation in the British war effort, and ensuring that nationalist Ireland did not appear, as a British side-kick, among the victors at Versailles.

Why had England lost its bearings in the world around 1900? Why did the prudent opportunism through which it had built up its Empire desert it? Why did it make that insane and catastrophic lunge at Germany?

I can give here only a very brief summary of the complex development which, it seems to me, subverted the historic political culture of England in the last third of the 19th century.

Seeley remarked that "a generation ago it was the reigning opinion that there is nothing good in politics but liberty", and that the Roman Empire was therefore not held in high esteem. But "the Roman Empire... is now regarded... as one of the most interesting of all historical phenomena" ("Second Course, Lecture V). And there is ample evidence that English governing circles from the 1870s onwards looked increasingly towards Rome to find their meaning. This was only partly because the British Empire was the biggest thing since Roman times. A more significant reason was that England had outrun its own political philosophy and could no longer cast its own perspective. It became a mimic. (What appalled O'Donnell about Curzon's conduct in India was the mimicry of Imperial greatness which replaced the empirical administration of earlier times.)

The turning to Rome happened because English Christianity ceased to be a functional ideological medium of real life for the English middle class which had become the central element in English political life as a consequence of the 1832 Reform. The old exclusive ruling class of 1688/1832 era eked out its existence during the 19th century, but after 1832 the conduct of affairs came to depend increasingly on the middle class. The English middle class was Puritan (or Nonconformist) in origin, and its entry to political power was accompanied by a great revival of English Christianity, and a simultaneous and connected development of the scientific spirit. The scientific Nonconformists had assumed that scientific investigation would confirm that the history of the world as expounded in the Bible was true. In the event, science proved the Bible false. That was a profoundly disorientating event in English life. There was no preparation in English culture for it. England therefore had to look outside itself for meaning. And English intellectual life became heavily dependent on German philosophy around the same time as English politics began to look back towards Rome. (And indeed the view to Rome lay in great part through Germany.) Rome at a certain point in its development supplemented its world outlook from Greek philosophy. The English Romans supplemented theirs from German philosophy. Germany, like Greece, was the land of poets and dreamers, and a successful political Empire might feel at ease borrowing from either. Except that Germany cohered into a very effective state at the precise moment that Britain was becoming culturally dependent on it.

I intend to show this development in detail in another publication. Here I can only assert it.

Delenda est Germania is a viewpoint which O'Donnell attributes to the Liberal Imperialists: *Germany must be destroyed.* This is an echo of the Roman cry: *Carthage must be destroyed.* I do not think O'Donnell engages in any exaggeration here.

But there is a twist to it. Germany was to England as Carthage and Greece combined. It was both the supreme rival and the source of inspiration. Rome could destroy Carthage without ruining itself. But Britain could not destroy Germany with impunity.

In the deluge of anti-German propaganda which poured out of the English middle class after August 4, 1914, there is a real feeling of liberation from thraldom. But, because of the inadequacy of English thought to English affairs, and the real organic dependence on German culture which had arisen in England, that liberation was a form of self-mutilation.

This seems to me to be the only adequate explanation of the British insanity of August 1914, on which the Redmondites staked everything.

The War Against Nietzscheanism

Redmondism was a form of West British nationalism as much committed to Catholic ascendancy as Grattan's Parliament was to Protestant ascendancy. The qualities combined under the description, "West British Catholic-nationalism" may strike the reader, in the absence of any representative literary/political material from that era, as being essentially incompatible qualities which could not form an actual combination. I can only say that a phenomenon combining those qualities was the main force in Irish politics during the decade leading up to 1914. I cannot doubt its existence because I have read its newspapers and books and have traced its actions. And I am assured that I have not misread it because Canon Sheehan, when reacting against it around 1910, described it in much the same way as I did when re-discovering it sixty years later.

Redmondism was superseded in most of Ireland in 1918 but it still flourished in the North when the present round of the conflict began in 1970. At a particular moment in 1970, before the Provisional IRA had become sufficiently developed to hegemonise the conflict, a body of nationalist ex-Servicemen played a part in the unfolding of events. Ex-servicemen's nationalism is beyond my comprehension. I have no insight into it. If I had not seen it, I could not believe it existed—as the man said about the elephant. It is an improbable combination of attributes. Here were people who were simultaneously proud of their service in the British Army and of their intense—even bitter—Irish nationalism. (Gerry Fitt—Lord Fitt—is not a perfect example of the type, but he belongs to it.)

This curious form of nationalism (which I find curious, no doubt, because not even a germ of it existed in North-West Cork around 1950) reached its highest development in West Belfast under the guidance of Joseph Devlin. Devlin was the organiser and leader of an ultra-Catholic society called the Ancient Order of Hibernians. The AOH honeycombed the Home Rule Party, making Devlin the effective leader of that too. The most brilliant of the younger Redmondites was Professor T.M. Kettle, who was an activist in the AOH and an admirer of Devlin.

Kettle, the son of a Parnellite Land Leaguer, was Professor of Political Economy in one of the Dublin Universities. His policy for dealing with Ulster Unionism (which in June 1913, at an AOH meeting, he compared to "a nigger minstrel band"), was to mobilise Catholic Ireland against it, get control over it, and then erase it by means of the education system. When the war started, he was in Belgium, buying arms for the Irish Volunteers. He immediately offered himself as War Correspondent to the chief Liberal newspaper, the **Daily News**. His article, **Europe Against The Barbarians**, published in the Daily News on August 10th, set the pattern for war propaganda:

"As for Servia, it seems probable that nobody will have time to go to war with her. Her function has been that of the electric button which discharges the great gun of a fortress. And now that the lightnings have been released what is the stake for which we are playing? It is as simple as it is colossal. It is Europe against the barbarians... The 'big blonde brute' has stepped from the pages of Nietzsche out on to the plains about Liege...

"And now we understand that the Immoralists meant what they said. We were reading, not as we thought, a string of drawing-room paradoxes, but the advance proof sheets of a veritable Bullie's Bible. The General Bernhardis who had been teaching Germany to desire war, to provoke it, to regard it as a creative and not a destructive act, to accept it merely as the inevitable prologue to German domination have proved to be not only brutal but formidable...

"I do not wish in any way to exaggerate. France has her corruptions. But the whole set of her thought even when it abjured Christian 'illusions' was towards solidarity, towards reasonableness and co-operation. Russia has her vile tyrannies. But from all Russian literature there comes an immense and desolating sob of humility and self-reproach. Great Britain has not yet liquidated her account with Ireland, nor altogether purified her relations with India an Egypt. But Great Britain does not, at any rate, throw aside all plain, pedestrian Christian standards as rubbish. In the Rhineland too, and in the south there are millions of hearty men and women not yet Prussified, and who still think it possible that there may exist a Being greater in some respects than the Imperial Kaiser. But all the central thought of Germany has been for a generation corrupt. It has been foul with the odour of desired shambles.

"The issue, then, is Europe against the barbarians..."

This is I think the original revelation that Britain was at war with the philosophy of evil, Nietzscheanism, which had become incarnate in the German state. The other leading Liberal paper, the **Manchester Guardian**, did not take up this theme until early October, when it was working itself up to a synthetic fury over the supposed destruction of Rheims Cathedral, but on October 13 it committed itself editorially to the view that Britain was at war with **The Philosophy Of Savagery**: "You feel the very breath of Nietzscheanism in the German Emperor's famous farewell speech to his brother at Kiel, with the "mailed fist" passage... The German campaign of barbarism in Belgium is simply *Nietzsche's* bookish dream of a conquering pitilessness put into practice." (The

24

writer of this editorial was another Irish nationalist, C.E. Montague. The editor of the Guardian, C.P. Scott, an old-fashioned Liberal, could neither bring himself to oppose the war after it was declared—though as late as August 4th he editorialised against "the participation of this country in the greatest crime of our time"—nor to enter into the spirit of it. He therefore left the writing of warmongering editorials to his son-in-law, Montague.

It soon became a commonplace that Britain was at war with a state which had been formed to give effect to Nietzsche's philosophy of evil.

William Archer, Bernard Shaw's colleague, wrote a pamphlet called **Fighting A Philosophy**. It was published as Oxford War Pamphlet No. 65, and is a fair sample of what was produced by British intellect at the highest level:

"Some people who profess to know Germany well are trying to make out that the temper of the ruling caste has not been influenced in any considerable degree by Friedrich Nietzsche... Nevertheless the exact agreement between the precepts of Nietzsche and the policy and practice of Germany cannot possibly be a matter of chance. There is not a move of modern Prussian statecraft, not an action of the German army since the outbreak of the war, that could not be justified by scores of texts from the Nietzschean scriptures. In many cases, no doubt, it would also be possible to find texts of an opposite tendency... But the dominant ideas of his philosophy... are precisely those which might be water-marked on the protocol-paper of German diplomacy and embroidered on the banners of German militarism." (p314.)

"He recklessly flung forth wave after wave of thought: those waves which were tuned to harmony with the pervading vibrations of the national spirit carried the message far and wide; those which were not keyed to the right pitch dissipated in space" (p6).

"A new philosophy may be a more powerful enemy than all the navies in the world." (p6.)

"That Nietzsche was a man of genius there is no doubt. He had flashes of amazing lucidity. He had a disintegrating intellect of such an abnormal power that at last it disintegrated itself... But one gift he never possessed—a gift most essential to the man who aspires to shape the spiritual life of the future— the gift of sanity... His attitude to life is thoroughly morbid, his reading of its laws essentially mad; and his mad philosophy was at once an effect and a very potent cause of that German madness which is convulsing the world.

"What a calamity that this national aberration should have found a man of sympathetically aberrant genius to interpret and intensify it! In a very real sense, it is the philosophy of Nietzsche that we are fighting" (p25/6).

Heinemanns, the publishers, advertised a book in the following terms (Evening Standard, October 7, 1914):

"**Nietzsche** by Dr. George Brandes. Carrying remarkable correspondence from the founder of 'German Culture'."

The Nonconformist democracy, which had lost its bearings and become dependent on German philosophy during the preceding generation, found this immensely reassuring. Evil was what it had known most about for a couple of hundred years, and now evil was rescued from the collapse of theology and placed on a pseudo-scientific footing for it, and the world took on a familiar structure once more.

Kettle also pioneered the "Hang the Kaiser" mentality which ensured that the Peace following victory would be no less catastrophic than the War. His Daily

News article, published on September 12, 1914, was entitled **Belgium's Cry For Vengeance... The Hun Foresees The Day Of Retribution**:

"Dinant and Spa are the latest Hunneries...

"The marauders still in Belgium ought to be given to understand that when the armies of liberation come back they will come not only to defeat, but to punish. If justice between peoples has any meaning, then somebody has got to be hanged for Visé. Somebody has got to be hanged for Louvain. All the other public crimes that have sent Europe shuddering back to barbarism have got to be liquidated in due retribution."

Erskine Childers, the overt British militarist and anti-German propagandist of long standing, shows up rather well by comparison with Kettle and others in August 1914. He did not set out, as they did, to debase the public mind and reduce it to frenzy. His Daily News article on August 8th, **The Battle area In The North Sea: The Problem Of The British Fleet**, is matter-of-fact. But the introductory blurb is interesting:

"Mr. Erskine Childers, who is acknowledged authority on war strategy and history, is perhaps best known to the general public as the author of the brilliant novel of naval espionage in the North Sea, 'The Riddle Of The Sands'. No living writer is so well acquainted with the area of the expected naval conflict."

Robert Lynd, an Ulster Protestant who had joined the Catholic-nationalist movement some years earlier and who later became quite famous as a writer of light essays for the London press, did his bit for the cause with an article entitled, **World Power Or Downfall: Germany's War Of Conquest**, which was published in the Daily News on September 10, 1914. General Bernhardi, according to Lynd, had written "Germany's fifth Gospel":

"He has translated the Manchester faith that mankind will be saved by competition in commerce into a Prussian faith that mankind will be saved by competition in bloodshed. He preaches this creed with an idealism which is none the less amazing because it is an idealism of perversion. He fulminates against peace as though it were one of the sins of Aholah and Aholibah... There you have have the insane gospel of Imperialism at its most muddled—the gospel of Nietzsche and Kipling seen through the mind of a Prussian man of action—the gospel that is now transforming Europe into the likeness of a madhouse on fire. It is the gospel of national selfishness—of cutting the throat of humanity for humanity's good. It is simply barbarism cloaking itself as the cause of civilisation."

Bernhardi and Nietzsche were the twin ogres of British war propaganda during the next four years. The only allowable question was whether they had poisoned the German nation or had been poisoned by it.

I have been familiar with Nietzsche since my youth down in Slieve Luacra—which has, or had, a German element in its culture dating from Young Ireland times—so I knew that what was said about him was gibberish. But, when I began to investigate that war propaganda, I knew nothing about Bernhardi. I read the books of his which were referred to by Lynd and others. All I could find in them is an attempt to show the powerful German pacifist or anti-militarist movement that it was living in a fool's paradise if it thought that Britain would stand idly by while German economic power in the world increased at its expense. The meaning of **World Power Or Downfall** was that Germany had become heavily dependent on the world economy and that ,if it did not acquire the military power and will to protect its economic position in the world, it would be destroyed by Britain.

Bernhardi was a retired Cavalry general with some diplomatic experience. He had an incisive historical knowledge of Britain. He tried to make the German public understand that Britain was a militaristic state and nation (a fact which I grasped when I first saw the Remembrance Day rituals in Whitehall over thirty years ago), and that it was a virtual certainty that it would manoeuvre to get Germany at a disadvantage and make war on it.

Shortly after the declaration of war, a book by Bernhardi, "translated by J. Ellis Barker, Author of 'Modern Germany'", was published in London in a cheap edition, under the title, **Britain As Germany's Vassal**. The title of the original German was **Deutschland und der nächste Krieg**: Germany And The Next War. There is nothing in the content of the book to justify the change of title.

The story of the Nietzsche aspect of the propaganda is even richer. As I was reading all that propaganda I remembered an interesting fact. In the mid-fifties in rural Ireland I happened to come across **Thus Spake Zarathustra** in the Everyman Library edition. I was very taken by it and consumed it in a couple of days. I saw from the bibliography that another of his books was called **Beyond Good And Evil**. Being myself very much out of joint with the good and evil of Catholic-nationalism, I wrote to a bookshop in Cork city and asked them to get it for me. I had often got books by post through that shop, but I had never been there as I did not like cities. I later discovered that the bookseller supposed me to be an elderly gentleman who had grown world-weary and retired to the wilderness—not the teenage labourer obsessed with sport that I was. Nevertheless, he refused to get a book with such a title. (If he had tried, he would have found it was not in print, and that he might have remained morally pure without sacrificing business.)

A couple of years later the religious condition of Irish society made it necessary for me to leave it. I went to London. One of the first things I did there was to get a reader's ticket to the British Museum and read the whole of Nietzsche. And, as I read the anti-German war propaganda, I suddenly recalled that what I had read was a Collected Works of Nietzsche. I went back to make certain. And there it was: the Collected Works in 18 volumes, published between 1906 and 1912.

That is a very remarkable fact. I know of no other foreign philosopher whose Collected Works have been published in English. There are Collected Works of Lenin, Stalin and Mao in English translations, but they were done in Moscow and Peking. But the Collected Works of Nietzsche was an entirely English enterprise, done by the English middle class to meet a need in English society.

In the 1880s Nietzsche had to pay a publisher to print his books as they only sold about forty copies each. His fame occurred first in France and then in England. He himself developed within the free thought which has characterised German culture since the time of Frederick the Great, but it was in French and English culture that he was needed—in England especially, because it was in England that Christianity had collapsed without producing a native philosophy to take its place. And though German academic life produced post-Christian philosophy, it was not in Germany that Christianity had collapsed as a medium of actual life.

England had dominion of the world but had lost the beliefs that animated it while it was acquiring that dominion. The middle and upper classes lived increasingly in the routines of power. The great battle for Darwinism had been fought and won in the public mind amidst great public controversy. After Darwinism came Social-Darwinism. But how might Social-Darwinism be forged into a culture capable of maintaining society?

The natural world does not read Darwin. Its instincts are unaffected by Darwin's observations and generalisations. It gets on with living as it did before Darwin was ever thought of. But such is not the case with a human society in which Darwinian theory is established by popular dispute against the resistance of traditional beliefs—and in England the Darwin dispute was a sort of referendum battle on the question of Christian belief.

Is the Darwin theory as applied to society also a form of belief that society can live by? This was the dilemma of English life, which caused Nietzsche's writings to begin to be published in English even before his death in 1900. His stylish paragraphs and epigrams on the convolutions of the will to power—and his poetry of the will to power: "In dein Auge schaute Ich jungst, O Leben"—which interested so few Germans in 1890, fascinated thousands of middle class English in 1900. That is why when English intellect sought to re-establish itself on its own foundations after August 4, 1914, articles, pamphlets and books on Nietzsche flowed from it in a great deluge. England had a great deal to say against Nietzsche because it had been so intimately acquainted with him—much better acquainted than Germany was. But its moral war against Nietzscheanism only bore out what Nietzsche had reported of his observations on these things. Its morality was a propagandist device deployed in the service of the will to power. Truth played no part at all in it. Whatever served to heighten popular feeling against Germans, and to sustain popular frenzy through four years of unprecedented slaughter, passed for truth.

Hitler, as a private soldier, observed the thoroughness of British war propaganda, which had no concern with empirical truth and conceded nothing to the enemy, and contrasted it with the amateurishness of German war propaganda which made some effort to be impartial. In **Mein Kampf** he sang the praises of the British war propaganda and took his own approach to truth from it (see Chapter 6).

Of course, lies are always told in war, but never before had such lies as these been told. In earlier times, the people who conducted public affairs knew more or less what the truth was and could revert to it after the need to lie had passed. That condition of things was abolished by the agnostic British middle class on August 5th, 1914. Truth became what it was expedient to say in the struggle for power. Lies were what the enemy said. And this condition was total and irreversible.

The Italian Prime Minister, Francesco Nitti, was present among the victors at Versailles in 1919. (Italy had joined the war against Germany in 1915). Nitti had not adapted to the totalitarian mode introduced by Britain in 1914. He had been a professor of Political Economy for a generation before the war and he retained an old-fashioned attitude to truth and lies. He was appalled when he found the major statesmen at Versailles acting as if the lies told in the heat of war had been true:

> "When our countries were engaged in the struggle, and we were at grips with a dangerous enemy, it was our duty to keep up the *morale* of our people and to paint our adversaries in the darkest colours, laying on their shoulders all the blame and responsibility of the War. But after the great world conflict, now that Imperial Germany has fallen, it would be absurd to maintain that the responsibility of the War is solely and wholly attributable to Germany." (**Peaceless Europe**, Italian 1921, English translation 1922, p33.)

Although Nitti "felt the deepest aversion" for the Kaiser and had admired Britain—"like ancient Rome, she was a truly imperial country in the security of her supremacy, in her calm, in her forbearance" (p13)—he was driven by what he experienced at Versailles to declare that, if Germany had won, the condition of Europe could not be worse and might be better: "Perhaps her terms would have been more lenient, certainly not harder, as she would have understood that conditions such as we have imposed on the losers are simply inapplicable" (p17).

Britain won the war and extended the Empire, but the imperial qualities admired by Nitti had evaporated in the course of the war, making it unfit for Empire. It had substituted totalitarian propaganda for lies in the course of fighting the war, and while that proved marvelously effective for war purposes, it rendered Britain incapable of constructive statesmanship after the war. And British war propaganda was the model for the Bolshevik and Fascist movements after the war.

I suggest that there was a kind of necessity in all of this. Britain in 1914 had become the most powerful state the world had seen since the Roman Empire. But it had lost its bearings due to the loss of internal coherence which I have described. Therefore, as the greatest state in the world, it became a catastrophic influence on world affairs.

France emerged relatively intact from the war and the post-war settlement, because its motivation had been clear and consistent throughout. It had fought a war of revenge and it acted with honest vindictiveness in 1919. The fact that it was revenging a defeat incurred by its own act of aggression in 1870 was of no moral consequence to it. An honest desire for revenge carries its own moral well-being with it. It is immune to the debilitating influence of the categorical imperative because it makes no pretence to being the lofty and impartial guardian of civilisation in general.

In 1919 Britain acted just like France. But, because it had consistently represented itself as acting out of a disinterested concern for civilisation, by acting but like France it acted entirely differently from France, because this is a case in which states of mind count.

Britain bears a unique responsibility for the scale and character of the war. It was a free agent in a way that neither France nor Germany was. The integrity of the United Kingdom was not at stake in the European war that began on August 1st, nor was the integrity of the Empire. The establishment of the German state had taken from Britain nothing which it already possessed.

Britain was the most powerful and the most pretentious state in the world in 1914. All that it stood to lose by sitting out the war was the Ottoman Empire which Germany was helping to consolidate. It is true that it had its heart set on destroying the Ottoman Empire and taking over a great part of it—and actually did so with catastrophic consequences for the Middle East. But it stood to lose nothing which it actually possessed in the light of day in July 1914.

By intervening, Britain magnified the scale of the war perhaps tenfold, and altered its character fundamentally. And it represented its intervention as being exclusively motivated by a concern for civilisation.

For these reasons, it must be taken to have had a unique responsibility to ensure that the war was conducted in a way that would enable European civilisation to be consolidated and enhanced by the Peace made at the end of it, and to ensure that it ended with a Peace at least as good as the Peace of Vienna (1815). In the event, the Peace of Versailles was, if anything, more dangerous to civilisation than the War had been.

The Great War was the war of the British middle class and its famous intelligentsia—H.G. Wells, G.B. Shaw, Arnold Bennet, A.V. Dicey, etc. etc. were in the front rank of propagandists in this most propagandist of all wars. And the Irish middle class of the Home Rule movement made high level contributions through Kettle and Lynd.

The democracy-at-large in Britain had prepared itself to do great things in the world. But it was wasted by the middle class elite in the worst of all Britain's wars.

The history of the war against Nietzscheanism has never been written that I know of. The patent absurdity of the ideological propaganda, and the catastrophic nature of the outcome, caused post-War British historians to seek refuge in obscurity. There is no great history of the Great War. And now that Nietzsche again looms large in English bookshops—with all of his works available in at least two new translations—I don't suppose there ever will be. But if you go back and look at the newspapers, pamphlets and books which told the British people why they had to exert all their energy to destroy the German state and chastise the German nation, you will find that it was just as I have described it.

T.M. Kettle had written a lively, well-informed Introduction to a translation of a French biography of Nietzsche (by D. Halevy) published in 1911, in which he said: "The duel between Nietzsche and civilisation is long since over... The crowd... has dismissed Nietzsche's ideas in order to praise his images... German critics have applied to Nietzsche, and with even greater fitness, Heine's characterisation of Schiller: 'With him thought celebrates its orgies'." (p7/8.) But, "it would be very superficial to suppose that a thought so passionate could be altogether unreal" (p18). Nietzsche was a useful antidote both to "Darwin, Spencer, and the English school in general" (p12), and "to sentimentalism, that worst ailment of our day" (p18).

Perhaps it would be too simple to take that 1911 article as proving that Kettle was a reckless liar when he told Britain on August 10, 1914 that what it was at war with was Nietzscheanism. I recall reading somewhere that John Dillon, who had English freethinking in his family background, was greatly disturbed by his feelings when, on a world cruise, he saw naked girls diving into the water around his ship when it stopped at a South Sea Island. In his recoil from those feelings, he became a sponsor of the Ancient Order of Hibernians during its rise to power in the Irish Party. And perhaps something of the kind also happened to Kettle with regard to Nietzsche.

Ireland Declares War On Germany

The Foreign Secretary's report to Parliament on August 3rd. about what he had been doing to keep the peace made it clear to the world that the Government intended to make war on Germany in alliance with France and Russia. The Prime Minister had already (July 30th) conceded (or boasted) that "this country... has no interests of its own directly at stake". It would go to war out of sheer altruistic .concern for "the interests of the whole world".

The Foreign Secretary painted a sombre picture of the situation. It was only decent that he should do so even though the enormous superiority of the Entente forces arrayed against Germany made a quick victory seem likely. But Grey admitted that there was one bright spot:

"The one bright spot in the whole of this terrible tragedy is Ireland. The general feeling throughout Ireland—and I would like to make this clearly understood abroad—does not make the Irish question a consideration which we have now to take into account." (Hansard. 3 August 1914, col. 1824.)

Ireland was sewn up for the Empire, and merited only those two smug sentences in the most fateful speech ever delivered in the House of Commons.

Bonar Law, the Unionist leader, who had been at the head of a rebellion only a week earlier, made a speech in reply which was very short and very much to the point. It takes up little more than half a column in Hansard, and consisted of little more than this one sentence:

"The Government already know, but I give them now the assurance on behalf of the party of which I am Leader in this House, that in whatever steps they think it necessary to take for the honour and security of this country, they can rely on the unhesitating support of the Opposition."

John Redmond, who expected to be Prime Minister of Ireland by the end of the summer, when the Home Rule Bill became an Act, followed Bonar Law. He said:

Mr. John Redmond (August 3 1914): I hope the house will not consider it improper on my part, in the grave circumstances in which we are assembled, if I intervene for a very few moments. I was moved a great deal by that sentence in the speech of the Secretary of State for Foreign Affairs in which he said that the one bright spot in the situation was the changed feeling in Ireland. In past times when this Empire has been engaged in these terrible enterprises, it is true—it would be the utmost affectation and folly on my part to deny it—the sympathy of the Nationalists of Ireland, for reasons to be found deep down in the centuries of history, have been estranged from this country. Allow me to say that what has occurred in recent years has altered the situation completely. I must not touch, and I may be trusted not to touch, on any controversial topic. By this I may be allowed to say, that a wider knowledge of the real facts of Irish history have, I think, altered the views of the democracy of this country towards the Irish question, and to-day I honestly believe that the democracy of Ireland will turn with the utmost anxiety and sympathy to this country in every trial and every danger that may overtake it. There is a possibility, at any rate, of history repeating itself. The House will remember that in 1778, at the end of the disastrous American War, when it might, I think, truly be said that the military power of this country was almost at its lowest ebb, and when the shores of Ireland were threatened with foreign invasion, a body of 100,000 Irish Volunteers sprang into existence for the purpose of defending her shores. At first no Catholic—ah, how sad the reading of the history of those days is!—was allowed to be enrolled in that body of Volunteers, and yet, from the very first day the Catholics of the South and West subscribed money and sent it towards the arming of their Protestant fellow countrymen. Ideas widened as time went on, and finally the Catholics in the South were armed and enrolled as brothers in arms with their fellow countrymen of a different creed in the North. History may repeat itself. Today there are in Ireland two large bodies of Volunteers. One of them sprang into existence in the North. Another has sprung into existence in the South. I say to the Government that they may to-morrow withdraw every one of their troops from Ireland. I say that the coast of Ireland will be defended from foreign invasion by her armed sons, and for this purpose armed Nationalist Catholics in the South will be only too glad to join arms with the armed Protestant Ulstermen in the North. Is it too much to hope that out of this situation there may spring a result which will be good not merely for the Empire, but good for the future welfare and integrity of the Irish nation? I ought to apologise for having intervened, but while Irishmen generally are in favour of peace, and would desire to save the democracy of this country from all the horrors of war, while we would make every possible sacrifice for that purpose, still if the dire necessity is forced upon this country we offer to the Government of the day that they may take their troops away, and that if it is allowed to us, in comradeship with our brethren in the North, we will ourselves defend the coasts of our country."

The leaders of the Empire were kind to Redmond. They ignored what he said and praised what he did not say. His offer to defend the coasts of Ireland from a highly improbable invasion by an alliance of his own Volunteer Army with the Ulster Volunteer Force formed for the purpose of resisting him if he attempted to govern Ulster was both bizarre and irrelevant. It was pretended that he had made a very different offer, and six weeks later he did.

The response on August 4th. to Grey's virtual declaration of war on August 3rd. was very different in the English Liberal press and the Irish Nationalist press. It was the English Liberal that opposed war on Germany. Here is what the **Manchester Guardian** said editorially on August 4th:

"If and when England joins in the war it will be too late to discuss its policy. Meanwhile we hold it to be a patriotic duty for all good citizens to oppose to the utmost the participation of this country in the greatest crime of our time. Sir Edward Grey's speech last night... was not fair either to the House of Commons or to the country. It showed that for years he had been keeping back the whole truth and telling just enough to lull into a false sense of security, not enough to enable the country to form a reasoned judgment on the current of our policy ...It is a mockery to throw on the House of Commons the responsibility of deciding at a moment's notice and in circumstances of excitement on a policy that has been maturing for years. Had the House of Commons as a whole risen to the full height of its duty it would have shown itself wiser than its rulers. But a minority did protest, and nobly, against the incompetence and secretiveness in the conduct of our foreign affairs, which now threatens to wreck the moral and material progress of half a century."

In olden times—in the distant age before 1912—the Irish Party would have been with the minority that protested. And with the addition of 60 or 70 Irish members that minority would have been a force to be reckoned with. But in 1914 the support of the Irish Party could simply be taken for granted by the Liberal Imperialist establishment. Redmond did not yet offer the nation as cannon-fodder for the war, but, in a frivolously Imperialist state of mind, he expressed the moral support of the nation for the war.

Nationalist Ireland, through its elected representatives and its newspapers (which counted for a lot more then than they do now) was thoroughly implicated in this worst of all England's wars. It was left to a handful of British politicians to oppose the war—the Independent Labour Party and some Gladstonian Liberals. Two Cabinet Ministers resigned in protest against the declaration of war: John Morley, Gladstone's biographer and John Burns, the Liberal/Labour representative. This British opposition was not supported by a single Irish MP. Nationalists and Ulster Unionists all supported this catastrophic Imperialist adventure and vied with each other to appear the most Loyal.

All of Britain's European wars since the 17th century have been balance-of-power wars. Britain has not been threatened by any European power since the 16th. century. (The successful invasion of 1688 was a contrivance of British politics.) A couple of years ago I described the balance-of-power strategy as follows:

"*Balance of power* means *divide and rule* in a special sense. The English strategy was to divide Europe in order to rule the rest of the world." (**Derry And The Boyne**, 1990, p39.)

Gladstonian Liberalism had developed an antipathy to balance-of-power politics. The Asquith coterie was therefore anxious to disguise the balance-of-power character of their war and to manipulate Liberal sentimentality by use of

moral red-herrings. But such disguises were unnecessary in Ireland. And in fact
The Freeman's Journal (the official paper of the Irish Party) stripped away the
moral disguises in its editorial of August 4th:

"Sir Edward Grey's statement...may be summed up in a couple of sentences: The
British Government does not believe it consistent with British interests or British
honour to permit a single great Power to dominate the whole of Western Europe
opposite the British coasts. To allow France to be reduced to the level of a second-
rate power, and the independence of Belgium and Holland destroyed, would be
dangerous to England. If supported by Parliament and the country the British
Government will, therefore, use all the forces at their command to prevent these
things from happening..."

"In the dark prospect Sir Edward Grey declared that there was one bright spot—
it is Ireland... This declaration aroused feeling. The feeling grew to enthusiasm
when the Irish Leader intervened in the debate with a declaration as historic as any
ever made by Mr. Grattan..."

There was no discussion of the merits of the Government decision to magnify
the European war into a World War. It was taken as axiomatic that the Nationalist
interest was included in the greater Liberal Imperial interest.

The **Irish Independent** editorial of August 4th was equally supportive of the
Government:

"Sir Edward Grey, in his clear and cogent statement...last night, established
beyond all doubt that England has made almost superhuman efforts to preserve the
peace of Europe, and that owing to the 'unmeasured aggrandisement' of Germany
matters have been rapidly forced to the issue..."

The following day (August 5th) the Manchester Guardian editorialised:

"England declared war upon Germany at eleven o'clock last night. All controversy
therefore is now at an end. Our front is united. A little more knowledge, a little more
time on this side, more patience, and a sounder political principle on the other side
would have saved us from the greatest calamity that anyone living has known. It will
be a war in which we risk everything of which we are proud, and in which we stand
to gain nothing...Some day we shall all regret it..."

The other Liberal paper, the **Daily News**, which had campaigned against
British involvement in the war even more strongly than the Guardian, also
supported the war once it was declared. It was a clear case of "My country right
or wrong!" Or even: "My country even though I know it is wrong!" But at least
the Gladstonians had used all their influence to try to prevent the war before
supporting it as an accomplished fact. Nationalist Ireland, through its MPs and its
newspapers, had facilitated the warmongering of the Asquith coterie.

It might be said that Gladstonian Liberalism put on a poor show in 1914. When
the crisis began to build up around July 25th the Liberal Imperialist coterie, which
from the outset was intent on war, had to conceal its intentions even from the
Cabinet. They controlled all the essential levers of power—Asquith as Prime
Minister and Secretary for War, Grey as Foreign Secretary, Churchill at the
Admiralty, and Haldane who, though now Lord Chancellor, retained informal
control of the military apparatus which he had renovated during his six years at the
War Office. They made detailed preparations for war without the knowledge of
the other members of the Government, not to mention the Liberal Members of
Parliament. At the start they did not see how they could avert a major Cabinet split
when it came to declaring war. But they pursued their object steadily and calmly
from hour to hour and day to day, encouraged by an informal guarantee of support

from the Unionist leader. In the event only two inessential Cabinet members resigned, and the Liberal Party in the Commons fell into line with remarkable submissiveness. And once war was declared those who had been anti-war up to the last moment became the most energetic and implacable advocates of total war against absolute evil as incarnated in the German state—Lloyd George being the outstanding case in point.

It was a miserable end for Gladstonian Liberalism. But it seems to me that Nationalist Ireland bears a unique responsibility for that Liberal collapse and for the catastrophe to which it led.

Ever since Gladstone had in 1886 made Irish Home Rule a central issue in British politics there had been a special relationship between the Irish Party and the radicals in the Liberal Party. Irish support for radical positions became the norm on everything but education (where Catholic influence aligned the Irish Party with the Tories). The alliance of the Irish Party with the radical Liberals was especially strong in the sphere of foreign policy. The total defection of the Irish Party to the Liberal Imperialist cause on the greatest of all foreign policy issues in July/August 1914 must therefore have been of immense value to the Liberal Imperialist coterie in depressing the Gladstonian spirit in the Liberal Party.

Asquith had the problem of averting a major split in his Cabinet, and carrying the Party with him, when he made war on Germany. Ireland was certainly "one bright spot" helping him to solve that problem. The Irish issue had been at the centre of British politics for two years. It had rendered Parliamentary government almost inoperative and had carried the state to the brink of civil war. But now both the Irish Party and the Unionist Party gave carte blanche to the Liberal Imperialists to make war on Germany as a matter of Imperial honour. They might feud over Tyrone and Fermanagh, and they might drill their respective Volunteer armies with a view to doing battle with each other over the enforcement of Home Rule, but they found themselves in perfect sympathy when it came to committing the state to an apocalyptic was on Germany. How could the remnant of Gladstonian Liberalism not have been demoralised by this turn of events?

If the Irish Party had committed itself against the war on Germany, as it had committed itself against the war on the Boer Republics, the outcome might have been entirely different. The problem confronting the Liberal Imperialists would have been greatly complicated. The Gladstonian Liberals would have been encouraged instead of being demoralised. And the Liberal Imperialists, instead of having Germany neatly blocked in and isolated, would have had to reckon on the possibility of Germany taking advantage of an exposed flank within the United Kingdom. It therefore seems reasonable to hold Redmondite Ireland jointly responsible with the Liberal Imperialists for the most catastrophic war in the history of Europe.

A further point needs to be made in that connection. It is that the participation of Irishmen on the British side in the Great War was altogether different in its political significance from the participation of Irishmen in the British Army in any previous war. In previous wars Catholic Ireland had no corporate existence. The British state, whether directly or through the intermediacy of the Ascendancy Parliament, had committed Ireland to war as a politically inert part of itself. It did not consult representatives of the people, and the representatives of the people had taken no part in making the decision to go to war. And the recruiting was done by recruiting sergeants.

Such was not the case in 1914. Redmond was not yet Prime Minister, but the Bill which would make him Prime Minister was within months of becoming an

Act. He was treated with considerable deference by the Government. He had a disciplined Party which had held the balance in power in Parliament since 1910. And he monopolised the representation of Nationalist Ireland apart from Co. Cork. His Party was an influential component of the state which declared war on Germany. And little recruiting could have been done in Nationalist Ireland without its active participation. The responsibility for the participation of Irishmen in the war of destruction against Germany lay squarely with the Irish Party.

The domestic conflict over Home Rule rumbled on for six weeks after both parties had made common cause against Germany. Although it had been agreed in late July that there should be a truce on the Home Rule issue until the German state was destroyed, and that neither party should be disadvantaged by the suspension of the internal conflict for the duration of the World War, each side naturally sought advantage in the arranging of the details of the truce. And it was in the nature of things that one of them would in fact be disadvantaged. (As Asquith put it on September 15th: "It is obvious to everybody that no party in this House, no party to this great controversy, can be put at the conclusion of the War, with all the unforeseen and unforeseeable events which may intervene, in precisely the same position as it was when the War began." Hansard, col.. 884.)

Both the Unionists and the Nationalist took it for granted quite early in the crisis that Britain was about to go to war and they began manoeuvring for advantage in this new situation. On July 30th the Unionists proposed a party truce for the duration of the war during which no controversial legislation would be dealt with. And on July 31st the **Freeman's Journal** carried the following editorial, under the title *The Shadow Over Europe*:

"That Europe is within measurable distance of a catastrophe greater than any that has befallen her since the fall of Napoleon seems to be the opinion of all men in intimate touch with international affairs... England is within the shadow, and affairs in Ireland have taken a new turn in consequence. Yesterday the Prime Minister postponed the consideration of the Amending Bill [i.e., a Bill providing for temporary partition: BC]... The Empire could not afford a debate at the present moment upon the issue into which the party par excellence of law, order, constitutionalism and Imperialism have introduced the element of physical menace and organised force. Thanks to these Imperialists the day of crisis has come, finding Ireland with rival forces amounting to two hundred and fifty thousand men at drill. The revolutionary action of the Unionist Party, threatening civil war, has thus complicated a question which by all law and precedent the Parliament is competent to settle. Anarchy has, however, to hide its head in the moment of Imperial danger, and the ordinary legislative process which is vital to the unity of the Empire is restored to its free operation. Ireland can calmly await the result. Her cause is safe. The cessation of the strife of parties is a measure of the gravity of the situation in Europe as seen by statesmen..."

The Redmondites felt that the Unionists had been wrong-footed by the turn of events, and they were jubilant. Not only had the Unionists introduced physical force into the internal affairs of the United Kingdom, and brought division to the Empire, but they had flirted with outright treason in their dealings with the Kaiser. An editorial in the Belfast Nationalist paper, **The Irish News**, on August 8th, commented:

"Only two or three years ago it was authoritatively declared in Ulster that the Kaiser of Germany would come across the seas, and as the head of "a great Protestant Power", help "Ulster" against the Pope and Mr. Asquith. The Kaiser did not come;

we do not suppose he was invited. But, according to the Unionists themselves, his Germanic Majesty was encouraged to bring about the present World-War by the representations made to him that Ulster was a mighty force, determined to wage Civil War if the Government of Great Britain and Ireland kept their pledges and carried their Irish policy into effect. Perhaps Sir Edward Carson tried to disabuse the Emperor's mind of this foolish notion when the pair held friendly converse last year at Wisbaden; but it is only too plain that if Sir Edward made the effort, he failed...because the Kaiser laid his plans for strife just at the time that Lord Northcliffe's elaborate preparations for reporting the "Ulster War" were attracting attention throughout the world. William II did not invade Ireland and declare war against the British Government and Home Rule; but the Unionists have resolved to use him at any cost; and as Home Rule was not killed by a German attack upon the coast of Antrim in support of Carsonism, the brilliant idea of destroying it under cover of William's "All-Europe" war occcured to the inimitable statesmen of the Old Town Hall."

And on August 14th The Irish News commented, under the title *The Kaiser's Ulster Lieges*:

"Throughout Europe, throughout the world, the name of the Kaiser is execrated to-day as the titular head of a brutal and ruthless system of bullyism without parallel in the chronicles of the world. But the Covenanters, God-fearing and Christian, would 'sooner be under the Kaiser than under the priests'."

On July 31st, four days before Redmond offered in Parliament to "defend the coast of Ireland" with his Volunteers, leaving the British Army free to deal with the Hun in Europe, the Irish News had anticipated that event:

"All the energies of the Irish nation, and all the resources of the Irish Race in our own land and the world over should be devoted at once, and in the most practical manner, to the work of making the Irish Volunteers an Army as effective as could be at the disposal of any small country. When 'negotiations' are resumed, the strength and efficiency of the Volunteers will be the most potent factor on the side of Home Rule. Tory tricksters are already preparing to take advantage of the situation with characteristic impudence and dishonesty."

The Redmondite view of possibilities in early August was something like this: The Empire was at war with the Kaiser, who had suddenly become the personification of evil for British public opinion. The revolutionary anarchy introduced into British life by the Unionist Party was no longer tolerable. The Unionists, morally disadvantaged by their dealings with the Kaiser, were obliged to return under the sovereignty of Parliament, where the Irish Party and its Liberal Imperialist allies were supreme. The Nationalist majority in Ireland was now seen to be the loyal and orderly part of the country. The Nationalist Volunteer Army would protect Ireland for the Empire leaving the British Army free to deploy all its force on the Continent. The local difficulty in Ulster would be dealt with after the war from a position of both moral and material strength. And the World War, though terrible, would be brief, because the astute statesmanship of the Liberal Imperialist Government had ensured that Germany was all but isolated and was caught between two massive armies, each equal to its own. ("The hope is possible to entertain that it [the war] may not be of long duration...The mere cost of it must rapidly cripple and exhaust the resources of the most resourceful of the nations. That Germany itself can have accurately estimated the cost seems impossible. She is in the struggle practically alone. Italy stands aside...Austrian co-operation cannot be reckoned for much." Freeman's Journal, August 5th.)

This view was very badly misconceived on all counts.

The reckoning on a quick victory, though apparently warranted by numbers and armaments, proved to be a miscalculation of absurd proportions. Instead of being over by Christmas, 1914, it continued until the late autumn of 1918. And casualties increased more than proportionately to duration. The casualties incurred in the first day of the Battle of the Somme were on a scale that was simply unimaginable in 1914. Even though the German state was caught at a disadvantage, the mad project of destroying it proved so difficult that the vast Russian state crumbled in the process and there were a couple of moments when even war-loving Britain was in danger of crumbling.

But the reckoning on a quick victory was an intelligent mistake by comparison with the reckoning that the "cessation of the strife of parties" was to the Nationalist advantage.

The flirtation of the Unionists with the Kaiser during the Home Rule conflict was not, as the Nationalists imagined, a point in favour of Home Rule in the *realpolitik* of the state. It enabled them to make moral debating points against the Unionists, but they misled only themselves with those debating points. The boldness of the Unionists immediately before the war made it all the more necessary for the Government to conciliate them upon going to war.

The Unionist leaders had based their extra-Parliamentary opposition to the Home Rule Bill on the argument that as a drastic Constitutional innovation it required more than the sanction of an opportunist Parliamentary combination to make it Constitutional. They demanded that the Government resolve the crisis by holding an election on the Bill, and undertook to abide by the outcome. But the Government would not risk an election.

The Parliamentary split on the Bill reflected a division in the country at large. That is why the Unionists held their own—indeed more than held their own—when they carried their opposition to the Bill outside Parliament. (England may have sought to foist formalist Parliamentary illusions on others but it never submitted to them itself.)

It was therefore out of the question that the Government should proceed with the war against Germany on a party basis. The Freeman's Journal was greatly mistaken in supposing that "the ordinary legislative process... is restored to its free operation" by the "cessation of the strife of parties" (the "strife of parties" here meaning the Unionist appeal from Parliament to the country). Even if the "ordinary legislative process" had been freely operating before the war, it would have been restricted by the exigencies of a war of peoples.

Parliament had functioned normally during the war against Napoleon because political parties in those times were little more than family combinations within the gentry and aristocracy. Fox could harass Pitt in Parliament while Pitt held the country at war, because the conflict of Fox and Pitt was not the apex of a great party conflict which functioned right down to the base of society. The conduct of the state was, prior to the 1832 Reform, the exclusive business of a very small upper stratum. That Reform made it the business also of the middle class. And subsequent reforms had by 1914 extended the franchise to include most of the working class—women of all classes being still excluded of course.

As the franchise was extended downwards the old ruling class undertook to "educate our masters". By this process of political education, largely achieved by the remaking of the old Parliamentary groupings of the gentry into mass parties in the country, democracy, which until then had been taken to be an infallible recipe for anarchy, was forged into an orderly system of government. But the effect of democratisation on the conduct of foreign policy was to make it an even more exclusive preserve than it had been prior to 1832. A hundred thousand gentry may include a sufficiently high proportion well enough informed about international affairs to constitute a force of public opinion exerting effective influence on the Foreign Office. But, when the electorate ran into millions, the formation of effective public opinion on foreign policy issues by individual reflection on them ceased to be possible. The electorate became something to be handled by the Party leaders. Issues were reduced to shibboleths. The opinion of the nation became unanimous when the leaders of the two major parties agreed on a shibboleth. And, by the same token, conflict between the Party leaders signified, or produced, conflict in the country.

The Liberal Imperialist coup in the Liberal Party, and the attachment of the Irish Party to the Liberal Imperialists, over-rode the efforts of the Daily News and the Manchester Guardian to make the old Gladstonian Liberalism into an effective force opposing the war. But by going to war the Liberal Imperialists and the Irish Party made themselves dependent on the Unionist Party. There could therefore be no question of establishing the Home Rule system in Ireland during the war.

And there is a further consideration, which must have been well known to the leaders of the Irish Party, that made their calculation of probabilities not only wrong but foolish. Asquith had, since the Curragh Mutiny in March 1914, been Secretary for War as well as Prime Minister. When Haldane left the War Office to become Lord Chancellor in 1912 he was succeeded by Col. J.E.B. Seely, who was perfectly attuned to the anti-German attitude set by Haldane. But Seely resigned in March 1914 because it was felt that he had mishandled the Curragh affair—in which a number of officers declared that they would resign their commissions rather than be used to enforce Home Rule on Ulster.

Seely was not replaced at the War Office. For four months Asquith was his own War Minister. That combination of offices was, I think, very unusual, and was a very curious combination indeed for peacetime, yet it has rarely been commented on. A biography published in 1915 says:

"At that extreme moment of crisis (on March 30) Mr. Asquith took the step which is perhaps the greatest act of State in his whole career. He made himself Secretary of State for War as well as Prime Minister. This simple act of taking charge—an act taken entirely on his own initiative and without consultation with the Cabinet—brought a sudden calm and hush to the storm. It cut the Gordian knot of the 'Gough memorandum', and the Seely resignation, and all the barbed entanglements of those weeks. The officers went back to their posts. There was a lull...

Then the lights of Europe went out, and the squabble over Tyrone and Monaghan to which, at that moment, the Home Rule quarrel had narrowed itself, gave place to a fight for the command of the world. So there we leave that drama of civil dissension—suddenly broken off in mid-action—never, let us hope, to be taken up again in the same spirit." (**Herbert Henry Asquith** by Harold Spender. 1915, pp. 135/8.)

Asquith himself gives no account of the matter in his **Memories And Reflections 1852-1927** (1928). He merely has the following entry for August 5th, 1914: "I have taken an important decision today: to give up the War Office and install Kitchener there as an emergency man until the war comes to an end. It is quite impossible for me to go on now that war is actually in being." (Vol. 2, p24.) And there is a footnote: "I had assumed the Secretaryship of State for War after the Curragh Affair".

The fact that Asquith held the War Office until August 5th. meant that during the ten or eleven days leading up to the declaration of war, when it was necessary to put the state on a war footing without the knowledge of the Cabinet, not to mention the Commons, the levers of power were in the hands of three men who understood each other very well: Asquith, Grey and Churchill. And that made it possible for Haldane, the Lord Chancellor, to take informal but decisive command of the Army on the basis of a chit from Asquith and, by making use of the connections he had established when re-modelling the Army in 1906-12, to conduct a private mobilisation (see R.B.Haldane, An Autobiography, pp274-9).

Secrecy is proportionate to numbers. And it might be that the addition of one to that inner group would have spoiled the game. Who might that additional one have been? Asquith, Haldane and Grey had been close colleagues for a quarter of a century. They had risen together in the hierarchy of the Liberal Party, and they had taken command of it together. In all those years they had taken only one other leading Liberal into their confidence—the defecting Tory, Churchill—and him only partially. Churchill was with them when it came to war and Imperialism, though not really of them. They could not in the circumstances of the time have taken some trusted Liberal Imperialist nonentity and put him in the War Office. And all the Liberal politicians who had made names for themselves and were therefore eligible for the office seem to have been of a Gladstonian disposition.

It would not have been prudent to have appointed a Gladstonian to the War Office on Seely's resignation. Such an appointment would have been very popular with the Liberal Party but would have kept the Army in an unsettled condition. Asquith had credibility with the Army because of his association with Haldane. He therefore pacified the Army by becoming his own War Secretary. I do not suppose that he held onto the office in the expectation that it would facilitate him in starting a war against Germany. Opportunities for war occur unpredictably, and war rarely seemed less likely than in the early summer of 1914. I take it that Asquith remained War Secretary in order to hold the Army together during the establishment of Home Rule government after the Home Rule Bill became law under the terms of the Parliament Act late in 1914.

The Gladstonians were kept happy with a suggestion that Asquith had taken the War Office in order to conduct a purge of mutinous Army officers and reduce the Army to a blindly obedient instrument of the Government. But no purge was attempted, and I doubt that Asquith ever had the slightest intention of conducting one. And once war was declared the spirited officers who had stated their intention of resigning rather than act against the Ulster Unionists—Imperialists with a strong sense of destiny—became the most valuable asset of the state.

Home Rule became a dead duck on August 5, 1914. The project of establishing a Home Rule government was essentially incompatible with the project of fighting a war against Germany. The importance of the Army in the life of the state was increased immeasurably by the declaration of war. And the Army was against Home Rule.

After August 5th the part allocated to the Irish nation in the Imperial scheme of things was to turn itself into cannon-fodder. And, in order to encourage the Irish to turn themselves into cannon-fodder for the Empire, Home Rule, though a dead duck, was floated on the water. On August 15th Asquith referred in Parliament to:

> "the great patriotic uprising of which we have had so many evidences in Ireland during the past few weeks, and which, as we believe, will bring, and perhaps for the first time for a hundred years, not merely those gallant Irish regiments who have always been in the forefront of the British Army, but Irish opinion, Irish sentiment, Irish loyalty, flowing with a strong and continuous and ever-increasing stream into the great reservoir of Imperial resources." (Hansard, 15 September 1914, col. 889.)

The great game of the Redmondites during August and early September was to get the Home Rule Bill on the Statute Book. The Bill had been passed by the Commons three times, in 1912, 1913, and 1914, and needed only the King's signature at the end of the 1914 session of Parliament to become law. Redmond had been dragging his heels on recruiting to ensure that the Bill did become law. On September 15th, Asquith informed the Commons that the Government proposed that "these Bills [i.e., the Home Rule Bill and the Welsh Church Bill] should pass on to the Statute Book, but, at the same time no effective steps should be taken to bring them into practical operation before, as a minimum, a term of twelve months, and if at the expiration of that term the War still continues, before a date to be fixed by Order in Council, not later than the duration of the War." (Hansard, col. 890.)

Redmond said he was perfectly satisfied with this:

"It inflicts a severe disadvantage upon us. But at the same time I must declare my opinion that, under all the circumstances of the case, this moratorium which the Government propose is a reasonable one. Of course, when everybody is preoccupied by the War, and when everyone is endeavouring—and the endeavour will be made as enthusiastically in Ireland as anywhere else in the United Kingdom—to bring about the creation of an Army, the idea is absurd, and cannot be entertained by any intelligent man, that under these circumstances a new Government and a new Parliament could be erected in Ireland.

Let me say further, and I am not at all sure that this moratorium may not in the end be found... to be of great good to Ireland...During that interval, Catholic Nationalist Irishmen and Protestant Unionist Irishmen from the North of Ireland will be fighting side by side on the battlefields of the Continent and shedding their blood side by side; and at home in Ireland, Catholic Nationalists and Protestant Ulstermen will, I hope and believe, be found drilling shoulder to shoulder for the defence of the shores of their own country.

"The result of all that must inevitably be to assuage bitterness, and to mollify the hatred and misunderstanding which have kept them apart." Hansard, cols 906-908.)

Home Rule being thus simultaneously enacted and suspended, Redmond issued a Manifesto to the Irish Nation. It was published in The Freeman's Journal on September 17th, under the heading *Ireland's Duty In The War*. These are the relevant paragraphs:

"A test to search men's souls has arisen. The Empire is engaged in the most serious war in history. It is a just war, provoked by the intolerable military despotism of Germany. It is a war for the defence of the sacred rights and liberties of small nations, and the respect and enlargement of the great principle of nationality. Involved in it is the fate of France, our kindred country, the chief nation of that powerful Celtic race to which we belong; the fate of Belgium, to whom we are attached by the same great ties of race...and the fate of Poland, whose sufferings and whose struggles bear so marked a resemblance to our own.

"It is a war for high ideals of human government and international relations, and Ireland would be false to her history, and to every consideration of honour, good faith, and self-interest, did she not willingly bear her share in its burdens and its sacrifices.

"We have, even when no ties of sympathy bound our country to Great Britain, always given our quota, and more than our quota, to the firing-line, and we shall do so now.

"We have a right however to claim that Irish recruits for the Expeditionary Force should be kept together as a unit, officered as far as possible by Irishmen, composed if possible of county battalions, to form, in fact, an "Irish Brigade', so that Ireland may gain national credit for their deeds, and feel, like other communities of the Empire, that she too has contributed an army bearing her name in this historic struggle..."

The dead duck Home Rule Act was signed by the King on September 18th. The Irish News of September 19th hailed it as *Our Charter Of National Liberty* and *Ireland's Magna Charta*, while the Freeman's Journal said it was *Ireland's Day Of Triumph*.

On September 20th Redmond reviewed the East Wicklow Brigade of the Irish Volunteers at Woodenbridge, and he addressed them as follows:

"The duty of the manhood of Ireland is twofold. Its duty is, at all costs, to defend the shores of Ireland against foreign invasion. It is a duty more than that of taking care that Irish valour proves itself; on the field of war it has always proved itself in the past (cheers). The interests of Ireland—of the whole of Ireland—are at stake in this war. This war is undertaken in defence of the highest principles of religion and morality and right and it would be a disgrace for ever to our country and a reproach to her manhood and a denial of the lessons of history if young Ireland confined their efforts to remaining at home to defend the shores of Ireland from an unlikely invasion, and shirking from the duty of proving on the field of battle that gallantry and courage which has distinguished our race all through its history (cheers). I say to you, therefore, your duty is twofold. I am glad to see such magnificent material for soldiers around me, and I say to you—Go on drilling and make yourselves efficient for the work, and then account for yourselves as men, not only in Ireland, but wherever the firing line extends, in defence of right, of freedom and religion in this war (cheers)." (Freeman's Journal, Sept. 21, 1914.)

The Manifesto and Woodenbridge speech of the Irish Prime Minister-in-waiting under Home Rule-on-the-Statute-Book, backed up by the Irish Party without a single voice of dissent, and built on by the Freeman's Journal, The Irish News, and The Irish Independent—organs of opinion far more influential than any newspaper is today—amounted to a declaration of war on Germany by Nationalist Ireland.

The Unionist Party declared that putting Home Rule on the Statute Book was a breach of the truce agreed in late July, which was of course music to Nationalist ears and was therefore of considerable assistance to Asquith in making them content with suspended Home Rule. Bonar Law, in the outstanding speech of a rather undistinguished career, accused Asquith of taking advantage of Unionist loyalty because he knew it was unconditional:

"They counted upon the public spirit and patriotism of the Unionist party here and of the people of Ulster—They said to themselves, 'Whatever we may do, they are bound in a crisis like this to help their country...'. It is not a pretty calculation—but I would like to say, with the whole authority of our party, that it is a correct calculation—they can count on us.

"There are two parties to this great injustice, as I think it: One is the Government... I have not at all the same feeling of indignation against the hon. Gentleman below the Gangway—not at all. The hon. Member for Waterford (Mr. Redmond) is not the head of a Government. He is not responsible for the welfare of this country. He is only doing what he has done always, putting pressure on the Government to get his own way, that is all. But I do say this with all sincerity, and I believe it is true, that the hon. Member for Waterford has never in his life, from his own point of view, made so great a mistake as the one he is making now. If he had allowed the Government to act decently in this great crisis he would have done more to help his cause than he will do by a hundred victories such as he is going to gain in the House of Commons to-day...

"We think there ought to be a truce. The Government will not have it. But we shall have it in spite of them, for it takes two to make a quarrel. Till the War is over, we shall, by every means in our power, help this Government because they are the Government, and because in no other way can we serve our country...Now, Sir, in regard to this Debate, I have made a protest as well as I could, and in doing that we have done with it. When I have finished we shall take no further part in the discussion...You cannot debate this subject without inflicting injury. We shall not do it. When I have finished we shall leave this House, and we shall not return to it till the subject is ended. We throw upon the Government the whole responsibility. We leave them to do whatever they like. But when the War is over they will find, or I am mistaken, that they have gained a Pyrrhic victory—that they have not in reality gained more than a scrap of paper by the way in which they have treated us today...

(*At the conclusion of the speech of the Leader of the Opposition, the Unionist Members left the chamber in a body.*)" (Hansard, 15 Sept., cols 901/2 and 904/5.)

The Unionists thus had it both ways, representing themselves as the injured party—as at the level of "scraps of paper" they were, even though Asquith in opening that debate conceded that, because of the way the Ulster Volunteers were rallying to the cause, "the employment of force, any kind of force, for what you call the coercion of Ulster, is an unthinkable thing" (col. 892)—while proceeding to acquire the substance of power in the course of the war. The movement which deposed Asquith in 1916 was led by Lloyd George, Bonar Law and Carson. Lloyd George then became Prime Minister in a Coalition that was substantially Unionist.

The Irish News was founded in 1891 as an anti-Parnellite paper at the command of the Catholic hierarchy. But in 1914, when the Dublin Nationalist papers followed the Liberal Imperialist line by automatic reflex, The Irish News behaved rather like the Daily News and Manchester Guardian, and gave expression to Gladstonian sentiments until the war was an accomplished fact. On August 4th, it said:

"Sir Edward Grey only mentioned Russia when reference to the name of that sinister power could not possibly be avoided... Most English Liberals dislike Russia; no friend of freedom or foe to brutal tyranny can love the Government of the Czar. These, however, are questions for British discussion."

And on August 3rd:

"The immediate causes of this most horrible of all wars in human history deserve recapitulation. In Servia a campaign of wholesale assassination against Austria was undoubtedly organised...The 'first fruits' of the conspiracy were the murders of the Austrian Archduke and Archduchess. From Austria came a demand for reparation, and for an ample guarantee against the continuance of the campaign. The Servians would have yielded had not Russia encouraged them in their policy of prevarication which culminated in refusal. Then Russia began to mobilise her forces. The Russian Czar—personally a mere cypher—was induced to address a telegram to the German Emperor praying for peace, and urging his 'brother' to work for peace; and the German Emperor was strenuously striving for peace when he and his Ministers learned that the honest Russians were mobilising all their forces—massing 4,000,000 armed men to strike at the heart of the German Empire. It was treachery of the blackest and basest kind—if the reports of the transactions are not criminal falsehoods. Germany had no option or alternative but to declare war: and so the struggle was precipitated."

It concluded this editorial with an interesting thought:

"When the armaments have been shattered against one another, the thrones based upon them will be cast down, and Socialism in one form or another will hold itself justified."

It would have been a serious matter for Redmondism if The Irish News had persisted in this attitude—so serious that Redmondism might even have survived the War. Though it was a provincial paper its attitude was of more critical importance than the attitudes of the Dublin papers. It was Joseph Devlin's paper, and Devlin was, through the Ancient Order of Hibernians, the most powerful leader in the Party. Redmond, the nominal Parnellite, had allowed the Party to be reconstituted as a thoroughgoing Catholic-nationalist party behind the facade of his leadership. Devlin was the leader of the conscientious Catholic-nationalism which was now the substance of the Party. He was also the leader of the Catholics in the region of the Protestant rebellion. Redmond could hardly have delivered the nation as cannon-fodder to the Empire if Devlin and The Irish News had dissented.

In the event Devlin became the best recruiting sergeant in Ireland for the British Army at war. The Irish News made the transition to warmongering by means of debating points connecting the Unionists with the Kaiser. And on August 10th it came out with a full-blooded editorial entitled *The Great Revenge*:

> "Ever since Alsace and Lorraine were wrung from France 43 years ago...her
> people have fondly cherished the hope of winning back 'the Lost Provinces' by force
> of arms one day. Year after year Frenchmen sighed, and planned, and wrought for
> 'The Great Revenge'. Is the dearest hope of France on the eve of fulfilment? All the
> probabilities point that way."

The Irish News neglected to mention that those provinces, whose sense of identity was uncertain, were lost by France in the war which it launched on Germany in 1870—the war which led to the unification of Germany as a state. But it is the least obnoxious of all the warmongering editorials I have read in Irish and British papers.

*

On September 25th, five days after Redmond's Woodenbridge speech, Asquith addressed a great Imperial war rally in the Mansion House, Dublin. The Irish News (Sept. 26) began its report of the rally as follows:

> "The entry of Mr. Asquith, accompanied by the Lord Lieutenant, Mr. John
> Redmond and Mr. Birrell, was the signal for a rousing scene, all the audience leaping
> to their feet and cheering continuously for almost five minutes after the Premier had
> taken his place upon the dais. The audience was probably the most representative ever
> assembled in Ireland, and included several prominent military men, clergy of all
> denominations, and leading residents in every part of the country of the most divergent
> political persuasions."

*

Irishman In Command Of Fleet: that was the headline over an article in the Irish Independent on August 4th 1914. It was accompanied by a large photograph of Admiral Sir George Callaghan with the King. But, alas!, Admiral Callaghan was sacked by Churchill within the week and was replaced by Jellicoe. And that set the precedent for things to come.

Lord Kitchener, an Irishman, was appointed War Secretary on August 5th. But Kitchener was one of those Britishers who were infinitely distrustful of Southern Ireland because they happened to be born there. (Another was Lord Northcliffe, nee Harmsworth, the founder of popular journalism in England with the Daily Mail, and owner of The Times since 1908.) He ensured that the Southern Irish who rallied to the cause of the Empire did not march into the machine guns as a national bloc of cannon fodder as the Ulster Volunteers were accorded the privilege of doing. Redmond's Woodenbridge statement that there should be an Irish Brigade composed of county regiments was ignored.

In the Commons on September 15th Redmond complained:

> "I appealed to the Volunteers of Ulster to allow us, shoulder to shoulder with

them, to enter on the defence of our country. I have got no response...The appeal I made to the Government [to act on the Volunteer offer to defend the coast] has met with no response. I must say on this question of recruiting that if the advice I gave, and if the appeal I made to them had been met, and if they had done something to arm, drill and equip a certain number, at any rate, of the National Volunteers, the recruiting probably would have been faster than it has been... It is unnecessary for me to tell this House of the magnificent material that the country has at its disposal in the Irish soldier." (Hansard cols 909/10.)

But since recruiting in Ireland was very satisfactory without according official status to the Irish Volunteers, and without forming an Irish Brigade, and since Redmond and his colleagues recruited enthusiastically even though their wishes were ignored, the Government saw no need to upset the Unionists or offend Kitchener by establishing what would have been represented as an Irish National Army.

There was no Irish Brigade. But there were "**Battle Songs For The Irish Brigades** Collected by Stephen Gwynn and T. M. Kettle" published in 1915. The nondescript service of Irish Nationalists in the British Army was compared, by Gwynn and Kettle, to the Irish Brigades in the French Army after the Siege of Limerick. They wrote in a Preface:

"Within one half-century, by 1745, it was computed that more than four hundred thousand Irish had died in the French service. The Flight of the Wild Geese had become as regular as the yearly migration of birds; but these migrants never returned... these memories must be recalled to help in realising what is meant for Ireland when for the first time an Irish Brigade is formed within Ireland's four seas in the name of the Irish nation. Their military oath becomes for the first time for Irishmen the true *sacramentum*—a sacrament of reconciliation."

Gwynn contributed a poem called The Irish Brigade, 1914. It includes this couplet:

"They fought for Louis, fought for James, for every despot's throne:
Shall we not fight who may defend a freedom like our own?"

Kettle had been writing war poems as well as war propaganda from the outset. A poem of his praising the Tsar ("A Nation's Freedom") was published in the Irish Independent on August 21, 1914. He was a much better poet than Gwynn. Here are some lines from his *Song Of The Irish Armies*:

Blood on the land, and blood on the sea?
So it stands as ordained to be,
Stamp, and signet, and guarantee
Of the better ways we knew.

Time for the plough when the sword has won;
The loom will wait on the crashing gun,
And the hands of peace drop benison
When the task of death is through.

Then lift the flag of the Last Crusade!
And fill the ranks of the Last Brigade!
March on the fields where the world's re-made
And the Ancient Dreams come true."

This literature for a non-existent Irish Brigade in a British Army that was playing havoc with European civilisation struck me as obscene when I first come across it. And it has not improved on acquaintance. Kettle's brilliance still seems infinitely more perverse than the brilliance of Nietzsche which he declared it to be the purpose of the war to put down. The least that must be said of Nietzsche's perverseness is that it was not bizarre. Kettle lured people to their deaths in pursuit of an utterly bizarre ideal. But I am aware that I see these things through the medium of the survival of Jacobite culture in Slieve Luacra in which I was bred. The authentic Irish Brigade that served with the French Army was still remembered in that culture, and you did not feel that the Wild Geese who served in it had wasted their lives. They lived a congenial corporate life in the Brigade, and they killed and died in a cause that was not a bad cause. The people who went off to slaughter and be slaughtered in 1914 did neither, and they are remembered with a shudder of horror.

But the evidence suggests that for a couple of years Nationalist Ireland made an earnest attempt to live within the culture concocted by Kettle, Gwynn and others for Redmond's non-existent Irish Brigade.

*

Here is the variant on Redmondite culture developed by T. P. O'Connor for the Irish in Britain. It is an extract from O'Connor's contribution to **The Irish In Britain** referred to earlier:

"When the Great War came, the time of test came also to this new relation between the English and the Irish citizens of the Tyneside. The Irish proved as eager as their fellow citizens to contribute their share to the defence of the Empire, and of the principles of freedom and democracy to which they had always given their adhesion...

[Joseph Cowen junior was Liberal leader in Newcastle] "Like his father, at once democratic and Imperialist... he felt that wealth was only useful when applied to great public purposes. He made a prompt offer of ten thousand pounds to equip three Newcastle battalions, one Irish, one Scotch, one Newcastle. The offer stirred up the whole city to patriotic impulse. It was fortunate for the Irish of Newcastle at the moment that there were in the city many men of their own race and of great position.

"The Lord Mayor was a sturdy Ulster man of business—Johnston.Wallace; his successor was also an Irishman—Alderman Fitzgerald; one was an Irish Protestant, the other an Irish Catholic. They were brought together by the common fight of European Christianity against the pagan savagery of Germany...

"...the Irishman in Great Britain occupies a curious middle place between the nationality to which he belongs and the race among which he lives. He understands and he supports with his time, his energy, his vote, his generous contribution out of small incomes, the struggle of his land and his people. But at the same time he understands the Englishman and the English point of view; he is able to see the difficulties which stand between Ireland and her aspirations in their entanglement with English politics and English conditions. He is more patient, more tolerant, more indulgent, if I may venture on the word, broader in his outlook than his countryman who has never left the shores of Ireland and never dwelt among the English people.

"This attitude of mind might have forecast to any clear observer the attitude which had been prepared for generations... Moreover, the principles for which Irishmen had fought all their lives were revealed to them, as in a flash, as the great spiritual and fundamental issues in the War. They had fought for a small nation; they had fought for democracy; they had fought for liberty; they had lived in a land where—whatever might be the case in their own country—the freedom of the individual and the representative character of the institutions brought home to them the essential spirit of freedom which lies at the heart of the British Empire. .

"They took their stand then promptly, without a day's hesitation, with ranks practically unbroken by anything but infinitesimal dissent. Meetings of Irishmen, larger in many cases than ever held before, took place in all the great Irish centres—in London, in Liverpool, in Manchester, in Glasgow, in Newcastle. At every meeting, without even a whisper of dissent and amid scenes of striking enthusiasm, the Irish in Great Britain pledged their support to the just cause of Great Britain and her Allies. For the first time in the history of the race, "God Save the King" was sung—because for the first time these Irishmen were ready to regard themselves as free citizens of a free Empire." (pp 27-33)

This, it seems to me, is both a truthful description of things, and an enhancement of the state of affairs which it describes. It consolidates a de facto situation by making it aware of itself.

The book also includes a section on *Irish Heroes Who Have Won The Victoria Cross*, as well as the King's Speech to *"The Unconquerable Irish"*—the phrase meaning of course that the Irish had finally been conquered and assimilated. An editorial introduction to the Speech informs us:

"On St. Patrick's Day, 1916, the annual distribution of shamrock from Queen Alexandra to the officers and men of the Irish Guards assumed a deeper significance for Irishmen, whose courage and resource in the great war shed a new and glorious light on the immortal story of their native land. For a number of years Queen Alexandra had personally defrayed the cost of a gift of shamrock to the officers and men of this purely Irish regiment of Guards, and at the ceremony on St. Patrick's Day the King and Queen were present on the parade ground, together with Lord Kitchener, who so soon afterwards was to find a resting-place in the all-embracing bosom of the sea. Ever since the final dissolution of Grattan's Parliament, the Irish Nationalist representatives had kept apart from royal functions, and the attendance of the Irish leader at the ceremony, together with the memorable speech of his brother, Major Willie Redmond, in the House of Commons a few hours before—in which the gallant soldier made an eloquent appeal for unity—was symptomatic of the epoch-making changes that the war had brought about."

T. P. O'Connor enhanced the pro-Imperial sentiment which had developed among the Irish in Britain. And according to O'Donnell he performed an even more critical task for the Empire among the Irish in America:

"Having mentioned Mr. T. P. O'Connor none too favourably, it is only right to put on record the signal service he rendered to Great Britain in the Great War. It is not too much to say that but for his eloquence and dogged determination to make English policy prevail, the United States would never have entered the alliance against Germany. Down to the third year of the War, in spite of such occurrences as the torpedoing of the Lusitania, the Great Republic resolutely held aloof and was forced to do so by the very powerful Irish element in its population and Press. So intensely pro-German were the Irish at the outset of the War that it would be risking something like mutiny in the American army, which has always been more than half Irish, to call on the troops to cross the Atlantic in support of England.

"To combat this state of things the British Government, by the advice of the other very anti-German Irishman, Lord Northcliffe, wisely sent Mr. O'Connor on a lecturing tour in the States. At first he was received with extreme hostility by Irish audiences and more than once risked personal violence, but he held to his guns and for over a year spoke again and again in every city and every hall from New York to San Francisco and north and south. He was backed by ample funds and propaganda literature—mostly lies. The American Irish were in large part won over or shaken, and though they voted a second time for Mr. Woodrow Wilson as President, on his distinct pledge to keep the United States out of the war, they had lost their solidarity and threw over their old friends, the Catholic Germans, a powerful community. The latter had, in due course, their revenge, and voted in a body against Mr. A. L. Smith, the Irish candidate for the Presidency a year ago [1928]. Mr. T. P. O'Connor was, it has been stated, offered and declined a peerage, an honour that was more than earned by his great services to England." (The Irish Future, p 67/9)

I cannot vouch for the accuracy of this. Hamilton Fyfe's biography of O'Connor is very inadequate in many respects and I know of no other. I also know very little about the A. L. Smith episode. But in matters on which I am reasonably well-informed I have found O'Donnell to be remarkably accurate. And it is certain that O'Connor must have rendered a very substantial service to the state to merit the dinner given for him in December 1923 by Curzon, the most self-important of the Tory Imperialists, Churchill, who was a power junkie, Carson, and the American Ambassador.

Charles James O'Donnell

Through the Home Rule Party nationalist Ireland became a willing participant in the British Empire in its greatest ever undertaking—a war of destruction against Germany for what Asquith's wartime biographer called "the command of the world". If the Great War had lived up to its billing by British and Irish propagandists, or if it had been won by Christmas, the subsequent history of Ireland and of the world would have been entirely different. Britain would have been cock-of-the-walk in the world, and nationalist Ireland would have been West Britain. But because the war advertising was fraudulent, and because winning it took ten times longer than anticipated, and there were days on which it cost 20,000 British (and Irish) lives, Ireland became independent and Britain declined rapidly into a second-rank power. I am therefore giving O'Donnell's account of the war at this juncture.

Charles James O'Donnell (1849-1934) was born at Carndonagh, Co. Donegal; was educated at St. Ignatius College and Queens College, Galway; took the Indian Civil Service exam in 1870 and was posted to Bengal; spent thirty years in the Indian service in Bengal as Assistant Director of Statistics, Magistrate, Provincial Superintendent, and finally Commissioner; retired in 1900; successfully contested the 1906 Election for the London constituency of Walworth; and served four years as a Liberal MP. O'Donnell, then, was a pillar of the establishment. But in the 1890s he saw that the establishment of which he was a pillar was beginning to crumble. His moment of truth was the appearance of Lord Curzon as Viceroy. Curzon was a pompous and grandiose showman of the new Imperialism, who gave India Imperial circuses while neglecting the provision of bread. O'Donnell, who saw the old Empire as the most useful institution in the world, was disgusted by this new departure. He was one of a group of Indian Civil Servants who retired from the service in order to show England that a great mistake was being made. In 1903 he published "**The Failure Of Lord Curzon: A Study In 'Imperialism'**", in which he said the Curzon "has it in him to do, perhaps, great things, if he could rise to some nobler ideals than those of a prancing 'Imperialism'." (p. XI) He was particularly outraged by Curzon's Partition of Bengal on religious lines (the source of the present divisions into Indian Bengal and Bangla Desh) and attacked it in **The Present Discontents In India** (1908).

In Parliament he functioned as MP for India. Britain was a democracy governing an Empire. He therefore required the British democracy to take an intelligent interest in how its agents were governing the Empire, and to take steps to remedy misgovernment which was endangering the Empire. That is probably why he lost his seat in Parliament in 1910. He was subsequently adopted as candidate for a Hampshire constituency.

He also took a close interest in the Irish University Bill of 1908, vigorously opposing the tripartite system of sectarian education which it set up—Trinity for Protestants, Queens Belfast for Presbyterians, and the National University for Catholics. In his Irish dimension he belong to the generation of Isaac Butt. (His brother, Frank Hugh O'Donnell, had been active with Butt in establishing a non-sectarian Home Rule movement, but had fallen out with Parnell, whom he saw as facilitating the displacement of the laity by the clergy in the public affairs of Catholic Ireland.)

O'Donnell was Irish and British, but he was not West British. He was Catholic and he was nationalist, but he was not Catholic-nationalist. He was a Liberal and a servant of the Empire, but he was not a Liberal Imperialist.

His account of the War is not written from an Irish nationalist viewpoint, in that his guiding principle is not that England's difficulty is Ireland's opportunity. His viewpoint is that of a pre-Imperialist Liberal who feels he did something worthwhile in the world as a servant of the old, empirical, Empire. What he sees is the bungling ideological Imperialism, which disgusted him when it came to India, now bringing ruin to the British Empire as a practical humanitarian institution, and also bringing ruin on other great states which had provided a more or less stable framework for the world.

The chapters reprinted in the following pages are from **The Irish Future, With The Lordship Of The World**, published by Cecil Palmer, London, in 1929, 5th edition 1931. The complete chapters are followed by a selection of short extracts from other parts of The Irish Future, as well as from **The Lordship Of The World: The British Empire, The United States And Germany**, first published in London in 1924. The Irish Future incorporates much of the material in The Lordship Of The World, some of it reworked.

The Irish Future with The Lordship Of The World
by
Charles James O'Donnell

How Germany Was Forced Into War
(Chapter IX in the original)

(i) "In a few years more the Tsar's Government would have so developed its railway system as to obtain a permanent and crushing advantage. With this consideration is very closely connected the hastening of the war." "That consideration, as we ourselves firmly believe, is what finally decided the German Emperor to make the war now instead of a couple of years hence."— Mr. J. L. Garvin in *The Observer*, January, 1915.

(ii) "The German army is vital, not merely to the existence of the German Empire, but to the very life and independence of the nation itself, surrounded as Germany is by other nations, each of which possesses armies about as powerful as her own...Germany has nothing which approximates to a two-Power standard. She has, therefore, become alarmed by recent events and is spending huge sums of money on the expansion of military resources."—*Mr. Lloyd George* in January, 1914

What "the recent events" referred to by Mr. Lloyd George were was made clear within six months. On the 3rd June, 1914, exactly two months before the war, the military correspondent of the London *Times*, Colonel Repington, in an article on "Europe under Arms" explained how well founded were German fears of Russian preparations. He pointed out that Russia had increased her "peace establishment" (!) by 150,000, making a total "peace strength of about 1,700,000, or *approximately double that of Germany*... next door to a mobilisation in times of peace." Yes. It was a real efficient mobilisation nine weeks before the War. It was exactly parallel with our mobilisation of our Fleet at the Spithead Review, two weeks before the War. "There are signs that Russia has done with defensive strategy. The increased number of guns, the growing efficiency of the Army, and the improvements made or planned in strategic railways are again matters that cannot be left out of account. These things are well calculated to make the Germans anxious." Rather, and within eleven weeks Russia had thrown 1,000,000 men and 3,000 cannon into East Prussia. During the preceding two years the great French armament factories at Creuzot had supplied Russia with 6,000 field guns, the famous 7.5's. The Russian Army was thoroughly prepared for the Great Adventure. So was the British Fleet. There remained only the murder of the Austrian Archduke needed to let loose Armageddon on the ignorant, innocent peoples of Europe.

In General Sir C. E. Caldwell's *Life of Field-Marshal Sir Henry Wilson*—"The

Col. Repington on Russian Mobilization.

Sir Henry Wilson (1864/1922), born Edgeworthstown, Co. Longford, was Director of Military Operations on the General Staff 1910-14 and secretly gave effect to the secret Liberal Imperialist policy of making military arrangements with France for a war on Germany. He was chief military adviser to the Government in 1918, but fell out with it after the War as he thought it was soft on Ireland. He had been actively involved with the Ulster Unionists early in 1914 and he returned to them during the Irish war of independence. He was elected MP for North Down in February 1922, and in June of that year he was assassinated/executed outside his home in London by the IRA.

man who made the War," as he is frequently called—it is noted at page 107 that

Six Years' Plotting admitted. Lord Grey in his *Twenty-five Years* freely admits that "several of his colleagues were entirely unaware that conversations between our General Staff and those of France and Belgium had been sanctioned six years before the War and had been *in progress long* before the Agadir crisis arose."

The first point, in fact, that must be remembered is that the War began in 1905 and not, some nine years later, in 1914. Before the former date, the Conservative Government had, indeed, made serious gaps in the tried policy of Lord Salisbury, which made goodwill towards Germany, if not actual alliance with her, the sheet anchor of England's foreign relations. *The Times* of the 8th January, 1924, wrote:

The Salisbury Policy.

"With Caprivi as German Chancellor and Lord Salisbury as Prime Minister the relations between the two countries were very amicable. The close *entente,* which had existed between England and the Triple Alliance (Germany, Austria, and Italy) since 1887, continued." "The fall of the Salisbury Cabinet and the formation of a Liberal Administration tended, *as always,* to bring about difficulties with Germany. The (German) Government was much concerned by the pro-French and pro-Russian leanings of Mr. Gladstone." Madame Olga Novikoff had taken charge of Liberal Foreign Policy. Count Hatzfeldt, the German Ambassador in London, reported to Berlin that "Lord Salisbury has shown the same confidence and the same openness as in former days,"—an honourable contrast to the secret "conversations" of Sir Edward Grey's diplomacy.

The following four paragraphs should be learned by heart by everyone who wishes to understand the origins of the War.

(i) **Mr. Winston Churchill,** in his truthful book, *The World Crisis,* vol. 1, p. 36 [references are to the 1923 edition, B.C.], declares unreservedly that "France, after her treatment in 1905, had begun a *thorough* military reorganisation. Now Russia, in 1910, made an *enormous increase in her already vast army,* and both Russia and France, smarting under similar experiences, closed their ranks, cemented their alliance, and set to work to construct with Russian labour and French money the new strategic railway systems, of which Russia's western frontier stood in need."

Enormous Preparations.

Please note the dates 1905 and 1910, and the adjectives "thorough," "enormous," and "vast."

(ii) **General Buat,** Chief of the French Headquarters' Staff in 1920, in an authoritative report to the French War Office, showed that in the spring of 1914 the French had 910,000 men in the "active" army, with 1,325,000 in reserve. "One may say, then," he truthfully declared, "that, without taking any account of the Belgian Army (300,000 men) or the four British Divisions, *France alone was at the beginning at least equal, if not superior, to her formidable adversary."*

Agadir Crisis: In 1911 Germany sent a gunboat to Agadir in an attempt to deter France from availing of internal disturbances in Morocco to extend its rule over that country. The current Encyclopaedia Britannica says it was "an event involving a German attempt to challenge French rights in Morocco". And it says in its entry on **Churchill**: "In 1911 the provocative German action in sending a gunboat to Agadir, the Moroccan port to which France had claims, convinced Churchill that in any major Franco-German conflict Britain would have to be on France's side."

Lord Salisbury (1830-1903), Tory Prime Minister and Foreign Secretary for most of the period between 1885 and 1902. He was strongly against involving Britain in alliances.

General Sir Frederick Maurice, Chief of the British Staff, gave almost precisely similar figures in these words: "In August, 1914, before the war, the French had 817,000 Frenchmen serving with the colours and 82,000 Colonial troops." Total 899,000, *practically double their army of five years before.*

(iii) **Mr. Gerard**, the American Ambassador in Berlin, in his *My Four Years in Germany*, p. 89, wrote: "Another reason for an immediate war was the loan made by France to Russia *on condition* that additional strategic railways were to be constructed by the Russians to Poland." That was in 1912 and Germany at once began intensive preparations. Her military backwardness before that year is shown in detail at pages 39-43. "The annual conscription in France was 50 per cent. larger than in Germany." (*Nineteenth Century*, June, 1913.)

(iv) *The Temps*, of Paris, easily the leading journal of France, in the beginning of March, 1913, recorded the colossal forces Russia was accumulating, "Within a very short period," it triumphantly wrote, "Russia will have 5,000,000 soldiers in the first line, supported by 15,000 pieces of artillery. It will be possible for Russia to throw 1,000,000 of *completely* organised troops across the enemy's frontiers within a week from the opening of hostility." A year before the War this French journal openly referred to Germany as the "enemy" whose frontiers were to be invaded and, in fact, were invaded before Germany declared war.

At the end of 1905 the secret "conversations" of Sir Edward Grey with the French War Office began. Then also commenced the evil policy of concealed alliances with France, Russia, and Belgium, "to which," in Lord Morley's words "Grey has step by step been drawing the Cabinet on." The first steps were naturally elaborate and urgent military **Concealed Alliances.** preparations by the Secretary of State for War, Mr. Haldane, which went on ceaselessly for eight years. Mr. Winston Churchill in his *Four Great Chapters of the War*, wrote: "The British Army went to France according to what may be called the Haldane plan. Everything in that Minister's *eight-year* tenure of the War Office had led up to this and had been sacrificed for **"Haldane's Eight-year War Plan."** this. To place an army of four or six infantry divisions, thoroughly equipped, and with their necessary cavalry, *on the left of the French line* within twelve or fourteen days of the order to mobilise, and to guard the home island meanwhile by the fourteen Territorial divisions he had organised, was the scheme upon which, aided by Field-Marshals Nicholson and French, he had concentrated all his efforts and stinted resources." "It was a modest plan; but it was a practical plan; it was consistently pursued and laboriously and minutely studied. It represented, approximately, the **"Maximum War Effort."** *maximum war effort* that the voluntary system would yield, applied in the most effective and daring manner to the decisive spot. It commanded the assent of almost all the leading generals. When the hour struck it worked with perfect precision and punctuality. There was nothing to argue about, nothing to haggle over. *The French knew exactly what they were going to get* if Great Britain decided to come in, and exactly when and where they were going to get it; and mobilisation schemes, railway graphics, time-tables, bases, depots, supply arrangements, etc., filling many volumes, regulated and ensured a perfect and *concerted* execution. A commander whose whole life led up to this point had been chosen. *All that remained to be done on the day was to take the decision and give the signal.*" On the whole the British preparation seems to have been the most

---

Lord Morley, John Morley (1838-1923), influential Liberal writer, author of Life Of Gladstone, Secretary of State for India 1906-10, Lord Privy Seal 1910-14, resigned from Government August 1914 in opposition to the War.

thorough in Europe—"the maximum war effort," "daringly" carried on over eight "laborious" years. How intense must have been the determination of the British Cabinet to "come in." "The French knew exactly what they were going to get." The British people were proud and glad to see the great military reforms of Mr. Haldane, but even the House of Commons had no idea of what were the secret alliances behind it all. The Earl of Birkenhead, with boyish delight, tells us the story of the hoodwinking of England in the following illuminating passage in a monograph by him on Sir Edward Grey in *The Sunday Times* of 4th June, 1924:

"Dangerous and Deeply Rooted."

"I have often amused myself by speculating what his reception would have been in the mad House of Commons of 1906 if he had informed the collection of hysterical sentimentalists *who kept him in office* of his conversations, at the time when they took place, diplomatic and military, with the French nation; and of the commitments *deeply rooted in honour*, if not in formal documents, in which he was gradually, *dangerously*, but rightly involving this people. The necessity, however, for such confidences, *did not*, happily for the interests of the world, *appeal to him*, and therefore for eight years everybody was satisfied. He and Lord Haldane, with the knowledge of Mr. Asquith, made preparations for the war that threatened; their followers made perorations on behalf of the peace which preceded it." [This article was published on June 8, not June 4th. Italics added by O'Donnell. B.C.]

This is a priceless picture of a trusted statesman "dangerously" and "deeply rooting" and "involving" English "honour" in a secret war alliance with France. His duty to his country and loyalty to his colleagues "who kept him in office," did not "appeal" to him. That is the deliberate judgment on Sir Edward Grey by a Lord Chancellor of England. No doubt Mr. Asquith, as Prime Minister, was even more to blame. A camarilla of three was driving England to its doom "step by step."

Mr. Winston Churchill was equally cynical and contemptuous of England's Parliament and of the electors of the United Kingdom,—the men who were to die. In his *Four Great Chapters of the War* he gloats over their deception.

"While the electors in the United Kingdom in 1906 were affirming 'by the largest majority within living memory' their devotion to the ideals of Peace, Retrenchment, and Reform, *their trusted leader*, Sir Henry Campbell-Bannerman, was principally concerned about the Algeciras Conference and had already,—always *of course* on the express understanding that the British Government was not in any way committed to war—*authorised military conversations with the French General Staff.*"

In his *World Crisis* also, Mr. Churchill laid stress on the shameless hoodwinking of the House of Commons. "Sir Henry Campbell-Bannerman was still receiving the resounding acclamations of Liberals, peace-lovers, anti-jingoes, and anti-militarists in every part of the country when he was summoned by Sir Edward Grey to attend to business of a very different kind." [p30. Churchill actually says "business of a very different

Shameless Hoodwinking.

Earl of Birkenhead, F.E. Smith (1872-1930), Tory Unionist, Carson's assistant in Ulster 1914, Solicitor General and Attorney General during the War, Lord Chancellor 1919-22.

Algeciras Conference, 1906, closed the first Moroccan crisis. France and Spain in 1904 agreed to partition Morocco between them, and that Britain should have Egypt as its own in return for its connivance at the partition of Morocco. The Kaiser in 1905 sailed his yacht to Morocco and there declared in favour of Moroccan integrity and independence. The Algeciras Conference left the issue essentially undecided, but recognised a French and Spanish right of policing in Morocco.

character". O'Donnell has quite a few inessential errors of this kind. B.C.] He quite revelled in the secret betrayal of the peace-lovers. The Cabinet was overwhelmed with domestic work, the Labour attacks, education, Ireland, the struggle with the Lords, the great budget and so on, a fact that gave Grey a free hand, and he used it freely to advance his anti-German passion. In his speeches there was a more than sub-acid tone towards all things German, which Mr. Haldane, with many protestations of affection for his "spiritual home," tried to disguise.

Mr. W. H. Masingham, the most cultured editor and journalist connected with the Liberal Press, in discussing Grey's un-English and anti-English conspiracy with Russia to destroy the nascent liberties of Persia and to drive out her American Minister of Finance, Mr. Schuster, wrote thus:

"Simply an Anti-German."

"The revelations of Grey's work at the Foreign Office contained in the book, *Entente Diplomacy and the World*, leave no doubt whatever as to its general character. Hostile to Liberal ideas, indifferent to liberty, deaf to the call of humanity, and careless of the peace of Europe, Grey pursued the end which, alternately schooled by the bureaucrats of France and of Russia, he put before every other purpose of British policy. He found England free. He left her anchored to the Continental system, and, as it turned out, fatally committed to the Great War. Whether or not he was sincere in his last overtures for peace must for ever remain a matter of doubt. That they were doomed to failure is a thing of no doubt whatever. A statesman cannot attain peace in three weeks when for eight years he has diligently prepared for war. In a sense, indeed, he had no policy. *He was simply an anti-German.* This fixed idea he pursued with little relevance to circumstances and with less regard to the interests of his own country. He would have gone to war over Morocco. In the Persian case it was not a question of going to war, but of destroying the liberties of a nation and, incidentally, risking the safety of India, in order to preserve at all costs the bond with Russia, which three years later he was forced to redeem in blood."

This is a hard judgement but, I fear, a true one. Grey was, according to his light, honest, but his light was the deadly darkness of anti-German diplomacy, "alternatively schooled by the bureaucrats of France and of Russia." "He found England free," after many years of successful Conservative administration of the Foreign Office. He left England maimed and dethroned from her old supremacy in European affairs. History can assign no other origin for the decadence of British authority than the secret caballing of Asquith and Grey with France and Russia, the two hereditary enemies of England.

Germany was not much moved by the Anglo-French Entente of 1905, which was the work of an exceptionally able Conservative Government, with Lord Lansdowne as Foreign Minister. There might be mischief in it, but Germany had great confidence in the traditions of Lord Salisbury, represented by Mr. Balfour, and even hoped that the *entente* might

It meant War.

have a steadying influence on France. The Liberal *entente* in 1907 with Russia, was an entirely different thing. It meant war, and the camarilla knew that and armed accordingly. Bismarck and successive German Chancellors after him used every endeavour to preserve goodwill with the Tsar's Government, and they were fairly successful. But after the quasi-revolution of 1905, due to its shameful defeat by Japan, the Pan-Slavist Party, under Isvolsky, took command of Russian foreign relations and, with the aid of Delcassé and Millerand in France, adopted an intensely anti-German

England starts Arming in 1907.

attitude. The British Government knew this fact in 1907 and Asquith, Haldane, and Grey strengthened the new entente in every way and proceeded immediately to prepare for war. Grey's speeches in the House of Commons threw a shield over their activities, but were listened to by small houses, almost empty benches, because not one Englishman in a thousand had any idea of the Devil's Broth that was being brewed by the camarilla. As I have said above, the French and Russian Press and the kept journals in Italy and other countries,—the bribery of numerous newspapers was never so widespread,—always wrote of him as an apostle of peace and wisdom. This ceaseless flattery in time told on a man, who was naturally modest and just, and he dwindled into becoming the mere mouthpieces of the French and Russian Foreign Offices, of Delcassé and Isvolsky.

During the four years 1906-9, when the fatal policy was finally adopted by England, I rarely failed, as M.P. for a London constituency, to hear Sir Edward Grey make his many speeches on foreign affairs, and to read in non-German Continental journals fulsome praise of his great qualities. He was the idol of the subsidised Press of Paris, Petersburg, and Milan. These speeches were thin and wordy. Seeking chiefly to conceal facts, they lacked the eloquence that only truth and straightforwardness can arouse. The self-admiration of Lord Curzon was almost proverbial, but, in a more marked degree, Grey's belief in his inborn wisdom showed itself in every movement of his argument. He was firmly, thick-headedly, convinced that under his guidance English diplomacy dominated Europe, instead of being tied up neck and crop in the Franco-Russian conspiracy against Germany. He knew, no doubt, that France was prepared for any adventure that might give her her revanche and again subject German Alsace-Lorraine and the Rhineland to the French Republic. He also knew, no doubt, that Russian policy was every year becoming more hostile to Germany, but I felt that he did not fully appreciate the fact that the vast Pan-Slavist organisation, the most active force in Europe, made war the essence of its existence. I had very intimate information from Russia at that time and it all pointed to the fact that the whole governing caste, military and mercantile, official and hierarchic, believed with intense conviction that Tsarism and the old regime must rouse the nation by a great national war or be strangled by a universal hatred. Nothing but war,—if England joined in, successful war—could divert the Russian people from destroying its tyrants. From 1905, when revolution made its first great assault on the Tsar's Government, the bureaucracy started on elaborate preparations for war, meanwhile keeping the wild beast of Socialism at bay by dummy Dumas and pretended reforms. It borrowed vast sums from France on the express condition that they should be used on strategic railways and French artillery. England, under Grey's guidance, backed the tyrants and we know the result

Not only did Germany studiously avoid all action hostile to England, but the Kaiser almost begged for an alliance. Lord Hardinge, in his "official report" to Sir Edward Grey of his long conversation with the German Emperor at Cronberg on the 11th August, 1908, makes an almost inconceivable admission of the intense desire of the Kaiser for goodwill towards England, and, if possible, her alliance:

The Franco-Russian Conspiracy.

Panslavism.

Kaiser Pleads for Goodwill.

"Towards the close of the interview the Emperor stopped me and said in a very emphatic manner:

" 'Remember that I fully adhere to and mean every word that I uttered at

---

Lord Hardinge (1858-1944), Permanent Under Secretary for Foreign Affairs 1906-10 and 1916, Viceroy of India 1910/16.

the Guildhall last year. The future of the world is in the hands of the Anglo-Teuton race. England, without a powerful army, cannot stand alone in Europe, but must lean on a Continental Power, and that Power should be Germany.'

"There was no time nor opportunity to continue what might have been an interesting discussion of a somewhat ambitious policy.

"On thinking over the Emperor's words and the general trend of his conversation, I cannot resist the conclusion that his last sentences were *the climax to which he had been gradually leading,* and that he wished to urge *once more* the greater advantage to England of friendship with Germany over the *understandings* with France and Russia, which have already shown such beneficent and practical results during the past few years."

That was in August, 1908, when Sir Edward Grey was so frequently denying to the House of Commons the existence of such "understandings." I wonder what, in that early year of the Anglo-Russo-French alliance, were "the beneficent and practical results" indicated. "Practical" they certainly were, if they refer to the "maximum war effort in the history of the British Empire" described by Mr. Churchill. The taxpayer and the merchant, the war-widow and the war-orphan, probably have other ideals of beneficence,—so, no doubt, have the Russian people. Mr. Asquith's Government may be confidently charged with having deliberately rejected German friendship and with having half-ruined the British Empire by an undoubtedly patriotic but historically ignorant and commercially idiotic policy of war. It is in this way great empires are wrecked.

A very striking confirmation of Lord Harding's "conclusion,"—that the Kaiser's supreme desire was peace,—appeared in the *Sunday Times* of the 20th May, 1928, in a letter from General W. H. Waters, Military Attache at Berlin in 1901. It is almost impossible to deny to this statement of facts the highest credibility. **"The Gulf of Silence."**

"I was present," wrote General Waters, "at the luncheon at Marlborough House when the Kaiser pressed for an alliance. The version of his speech, for publication in the *Court Circular* of the following morning, was compiled hurriedly in the evening at Windsor by various hands so as to be in time for press. It was, as the Ambassador, the late Sir Frank Lascelles who was present at luncheon, told me, a poor production. Sir Frank wished the Emperor to publish a full report of the speech, as it was such *a statesmanlike effort to ensure peace and a reduction of armaments.* William II replied that, as he was King Edward's guest at the time of its utterance, the consent of the British Government must first be obtained."

"This consent was withheld, and the Kaiser *wrote to me* that 'it would have been a deplorable want of tact on my part if I had caused the publication in German papers, as was suggested to me from different quarters. So my words were swallowed up in the gulf of silence, and the British people, to whom they appealed, never heard of them.' "

These words of the German Emperor should be made known in every Foreign Office in Europe. The refusal of the British Government to publish the speech at the time was an act of obscurantist ill-will that almost passes belief.

The camarilla, that secretly dominated English foreign policy, without the knowledge of the English people, had adopted the summary policy, *Delenda est Germania,* and worked for it ceaselessly and with untiring energy. The signal for war was given by the Admiralty despatching the Fleet to its "war station" on the German sea coast on the 29th July, 1914, without the authority and, indeed, without the **The First Overt Act of War.**

55

knowledge of the British Parliament, which on that day was in session at the Palace of Westminster. This advance of the British Fleet was the first overt act of war in the Great War and history must recognise the fact. "The French knew exactly what they were going to get." They had known it for years.

Mr. Churchill's account of the Cabinet meetings in the week beginning Monday, the 27th July, given at pages 193-217 in his *World Crisis* is invaluable. He definitely states that "the Cabinet was overwhelmingly pacific. At least three-quarters of its members were determined not to be drawn **"Overwhelmingly** into a European quarrel, unless Great Britain were herself **Pacific."** attacked, which was not likely." Then he describes the dogged assault by himself and Sir Edward Grey on this resolution, including the opening up, through Mr. F. E. Smith and Sir Edward Carson, of secret, unauthorized communications with the Conservative leaders, again without the knowledge or consent of the Cabinet. "At the Cabinet of Saturday, the 1st August," he continues, "I demanded the immediate calling out of the Fleet Reserves and the completion of our naval preparations." "The Cabinet took the view that this step was not necessary for our safety, and I did not succeed in **The Final Meeting** procuring their assent." But this step was necessary to **of the Camarilla.** make sure of bringing England into the War. Mr. Churchill then relates how at a secret meeting of the war camarilla, Asquith, Grey, and Haldane, at 10 Downing Street, he announced to it that "I intended instantly to mobilize the Fleet *notwithstanding* the Cabinet decision.... The Prime Minister... said not a single word.... As I walked down the steps of Downing Street with Sir Edward Grey, he said to me, "You should know that I have just... told Cambon that we shall not allow the German Fleet to **The Constitution** come into the Channel." [p217.] This crucial decision, **Disregarded.** though communicated to the French Ambassador, was reached without the knowledge of the Cabinet. The two men were deadly afraid that their long-laid plans might "gang agley." They pushed the British Empire into war without the consent of their colleagues or of Parliament. The great Fleet went forth to war in entire disregard of the British Constitution and of the wishes of the British people, "eighteen miles of warships" Mr. Churchill tells us, "running at high speed and in absolute blackness through the narrow straits" into the German Ocean. Armageddon was let loose and England dethroned from her primacy. Mrs. Asquith has described Winston Churchill's joy next day as he skipped down the stair-case at Downing Street, after the official declaration of war by the Cabinet.

Messrs. Asquith, Grey, Haldane, and Churchill have an excellent excuse for their action, but not for their secrecy, indeed secretiveness. They honestly **"We Have** believed that they were carrying out England's traditional policy **Always** of the Balance of Power. *The Times* of the 4th December, 1914, **Fought."** tells us

---

Mrs. Asquith (1864-1945), Margot Asquith, the wife of the Prime Minister. I assume this reference is in her Autobiography, but I could not find a copy of it in Belfast. There is, however, no doubt about Churchill's delight in the declaration of war. Martin Gilbert in his massive Churchill biography quotes Lloyd George's account, as recorded by Margot Asquith in her Diary, of Churchill's demeanour on the night of August 4th, just after he had given the order to the Navy: "Commence hostilities at once with Germany." It reminds one of how a bride was supposed to look on her wedding night. (Churchill's bride, however, had to submit a written request well in advance when she wanted to sleep with him): "Winston dashed into the Cabinet Room radiant, his face bright, his manner keen, one word pouring out on another how he was going to send telegrams to the Mediterranean, the North Sea, and God knows where. You could see he was a really happy man" (Vol. 3, p31).

"We are not concerned to deny the charge. The balance of power is to-day, as it has been since the days of the Tudors, a main factor of our policy....We undoubtedly supported the Entente to preserve that balance and to prevent the hegemony of any single Power in Europe.... The maintenance of our supremacy at sea and of the balance of power were amongst the foundations of our traditional policy. We have always fought for the balance of power. We are fighting for it to-day."

There you have the Imperialist will-o'-the-wisp. I don't argue that it was a bad policy, but the hegemony, the best the world has ever known, that was smashed, never, I fear, to be rebuilt, was the world-wide predominance **Our Money** of the British Empire. When a nation makes it its policy to **on the** cabal against and form alliances against every other nation **Wrong Horse.** that shows signs of strength, it is also making war an absolute certainty. The policy of Germany was the Triple Alliance of the three Emperors of Russia, Germany, and Austria, the famous *Drei Kaiser Bund*, the *sole* object of which was peace, which it maintained for nearly half a century. France holds the hegemony of Europe at the present hour and, in our semi-bankruptcy, we must acquiesce in it or go back to our old and tried alliance with Germany. Once again, in Lord Salisbury's wise saying, we put our money on the wrong horse. I can imagine my critics saying that it is unpatriotic to make such statements, but I hold that it is far worse to allow the so-called Liberal Imperialists to pose as the saviours of their country, which has suffered so cruelly from the secret, unconstitutional and mischievous methods and from the short-sightedness and ignorance of Mr. Asquith's inner Cabinet. England never again can be the greatest Power in the world, except by the renewal of her ancient friendship with Germany.

In the beginning of this chapter I have quoted *The World Crisis*, by Mr. Winston Churchill, as showing how as early as 1905 France "had begun a thorough military reorganisation" and how Russia in 1910 **"France** "made an enormous increase in her already vast army." Mr. **had not a** Churchill justifies these war-like preparations by a rather **Good Case."** feeble reference to their "treatment" by Germany. France had no doubt to accept a diplomatic defeat at the hands of Germany, but, as Mr. Churchill honestly admits, she was in the wrong. "Early in 1905," he wrote, "a French mission arrived in Fez. Their language and *actions* seemed to show an intention of treating Morocco as a French Protectorate, thereby ignoring the *international* obligations of the Treaty of Madrid,"—the first treaty. "The Sultan of Morocco appealed to Germany, which was enabled to advance as the champion of an international agreement, which France was violating." [p31.] Why was not Sir Edward Grey the champion? *"France had not a good case,"* but Sir Edward Grey and Sir H. Campbell-Bannerman contemplated war in her support.

In April, 1904, two treaties were made by the Governments of France, Spain, and England in regard to Morocco. The first assured the world, which of course included Germany, that the integrity of Morocco would be **A Secret** maintained and the policy of the "open door" would be applied **Treaty.** to the trade of all nations. Germany was unmoved, but in 1905 it was discovered, to the horror of the diplomatic world of Europe, that there was a second and secret treaty, which gave Morocco over to the entire dominion of France, whilst England obtained the absolute supremacy in Egypt. The trade door was also barred against other nations, including Germany, which most justly and most reasonably protested. The French Chamber of Deputies strongly condemned this worse than back-door diplomacy and the Foreign Minister, M. Delcassé, was forced by French public opinion to resign. This secret war-breeding treaty was not very creditable to either of the "high contracting powers,"—indeed, a shameful scrap of paper.

As to the "treatment" of Russia by Germany, it was certainly the most monumental idiocy in history. In his solicitude for his youthful nephew, the Kaiser pledged his Imperial word that, whilst Russia was at grips with Japan in the East, the power of Germany would protect the interests of Russia in Europe. A peace-loving fool. In 1905 the German armies could have overrun Russia and France, whilst England had not begun her preparations for war. And every crack-brained Jingo in England will tell you that hell is not hot enough for the murderous Wilhelm.

A Peace-loving Fool.

As early as the 8th March, 1915, *The Times*, at that time under Lord Northcliffe's control, and, in a special degree, the organ of the British Government, anticipated Mr. Winston Churchill's frank confessions of England's great combination with France and Russia against the German Empire. Scornfully rejecting the official myth that Britain had only intervened through solicitude for Belgium, *The Times*, now that it had done its work and justified the war in the eyes of the English people, blandly declared that the Great War had never had anything to do with Belgium or the Belgians. Had there never been a Belgium, England would have joined France and Russia against Germany all the same. In the following words *The Times* avowed the real reasons in an article entitled "Why we are at War":

The Official Myth.

"There are still, it seems, some Englishmen and Englishwomen who greatly err as to the lessons that have forced England to draw the sword.... [They know that it was Germany's flagrant violation of Belgian neutrality which filled the cup of her indignation and made her people insist upon war.] They do not reflect that our honour and our *interest* must have compelled us to join France and Russia, even if Germany *had scrupulously respected the rights of her small neighbours* [and had sought to hack her way into France through the Eastern fortresses.] The German Chancellor has insisted more than once upon this truth. He has fancied, apparently, that he was making an argumentative point against us by establishing it. That, like so much more, only shows his complete misunderstanding of our attitude and of our character.... Herr von Bethmann Hollweg is quite right. Even had Germany not invaded Belgium, honour and *interest* would have united us with France. We had refused, it is true, to give her or Russia any binding pledge up to the last moment. We had, however, *led both to understand* that, if they were unjustly attacked (!!!) they might rely upon our aid. *This understanding had been the pivot of the European policy followed by the three Powers....* If England had slunk away from her partners in the hour of danger, on the pretext that we had not given a technical promise to our friends, we should never have friends again." [I have filled in some of the parts omitted by O'Donnell: B.C.]

It is not easy to see how the "honour" of England was involved. History will, I am inclined to think, decide that her honour, and perhaps her interest also, bound her rather to her three-century-old ally and peace rather than to her old and, indeed, present enemy and war. The Liberal Imperialist camarilla decided otherwise, and England has lost a million of her sons and ten thousand millions of her wealth, besides her trade and prestige.

It has often struck me as almost inexplicable how experienced, honourable and patriotic men, as British Statesmen generally are, could have been guilty of the utter folly of antagonizing Germany, her best friend. For centuries, whenever England was in difficulties, Germany or rather Prussia came to her aid. I am looking at this question

England's best Friend.

quite cold-bloodedly, absolutely free from prejudice. My feelings are, no doubt, rather kindly towards the Austrian and the South German, but they are certainly anti-Prussian. I do not forget that the first use Prince Bismarck made of his vast power, after the defeat of France in 1871, was a venomous attack on the Catholic Church in Germany by his foolish *Kulturkampf*, which, though it imprisoned many bishops, also created the great Centre Party which has dominated German politics ever since. After the collapse of Prussian Junkerdom in the end of 1918, Catholics, Kuno, Wirth, Stegerwald, Erzberger, Marx and others directed German affairs. Prussia's treatment of Catholic Poland was modelled on the same lines as Lord Carson's attitude to Catholics in Ulster, that is, as a helot race. Prussia has no attraction for an Irish Catholic, but she was the truest ally England ever had, and the most reliable. Her enemies were England's enemies. Canada would be a great French Dominion at the present hour, and France would have been the dominant Power in India but for Prussia.

The Hon. J. W. Fortescue, *The Times* military correspondent, in July 1908, before we had begun to lie about everything connected with Germany, wrote:

"The great successes and the material gains of England during the war were mainly due to this policy"—('the whole-hearted alliance with Prussia during the Seven Years War'). "The influence of the continental pressure upon British fortunes was strongly **Canada** marked. French troops and French revenue became more and **and India.** more engaged each year in the continental war, and both the French Navy and the French colonies were first starved and then abandoned to their fate. When Montcalm pleaded for support to enable him to withstand the attack which eventually destroyed French predominance in Canada, he was answered in February 1759, that it was necessary for France to concentrate the whole strength of the kingdom for a decisive operation in Europe, and therefore the aid required cannot be sent. It was the same in India, where Lally, after a gallant struggle, was overwhelmed for want of support. It was the same in the West Indies and in West Africa. The absorption of France in continental wars caused her to begin the war insufficiently armed at sea and in her distant possessions, and the same cause denied her the power of recovering herself during the campaign."

There is the plain truth. England as a Colonial Power owed her greatest over-sea conquests to Prussian aid. Waterloo also would have been a Fontenoy but for Blucher's brave battalions struggling through the night to come to Wellington's assistance. *Vorwarts, meine Kinder*, "On, on, my children" to England's help was the cry of the old Marshal, a man of seventy, as, refusing to ride his charger, he marched on foot at the head of his veterans. There has been deep ingratitude.

Even immediately before the war the average German could not believe that England was his enemy. Men like Von Tirpitz and Hindenberg sent their sons to Oxford and Eton. Vicious anti-Germans have been telling us for years that the "Boches" looked forward to the day,—*der Tag*,—when they would destroy the British Empire. Those who read the German Press, as I did, know that *der Tag* meant the day when they would throw back the Franco- **Der Tag** Russian assault and free Germany once and for ever from **Real Meaning.** the terrible perils he knew to be hanging over her, two simultaneous invasions from west and east. They came in 1914 and, but for England's insane misreading of history, they would both have been repulsed.

Fontenoy (1745), a French victory over the Allied armies of Britain, Holland, Austria, and Hanover, of which the centrepiece was a charge by the Irish Brigade against the British line.

Germany Peaceful And Unprepared Before 1912
(Chapter X in original)

German Humanity.

(i) "The artillery with its out-of-date guns and slow and ineffective methods of fire appeared so inferior that it can have no pretension to measure itself against the French on anything approaching level terms."

"The nation, which after all gives up little more than half its able-bodied sons to the army, has become less militarist than formerly."—Col. Repington, Military Correspondent, in *The Times* of 28th October, 1911.

(ii) "How great the neglect of the German Army has been and how insufficient its strength can be shown to any layman. The annual conscription in France is fifty per cent. larger than in Germany in proportion to population."—Mr. Ellis Barker, the very eminent publicist, in *The Nineteenth Century* of June, 1913.

Both these writers were notoriously anti-German and wrote after repeated visits to Germany. The former witnessed the manoeuvres in Prussia in 1911.

After 1871 United Germany settled herself down to the arts of peace, first reducing her army to less than pre-war strength, whilst France strained every nerve to rebuild her shattered forces. It was not till 1904, after thirty-three years, a third of a century, of peaceful development, that at last the threatening military activity of France, urged on by the Revenge (*Revanche*) Party, forced Germany to raise her army to the numbers of that of France. The *Statesman's Year Book* makes this quite plain. I quote the following figures from this most thorough and reliable publication. It is impossible to challenge the accuracy of any one of them. The French Assembly passed a law in 1886 raising the French Army on a peace footing to 500,000 men. The German Army in that year numbered 427,000. Any increase was furiously opposed and prevented by the Liberals in the Reichsrat. It was not till the Reichsrat had been dissolved and re-elected that in 1893 the German Army was increased to 479,000 men, in 1899 to 495,000, and at last in 1904 to 505,000. Forthwith France increased to 545,000. No nation had to complain of German encroachments. She sought no conquests in Europe, but by the Three Kaiser Alliance with Russia and Austria laboured to maintain the peace of the world. Her relations with Italy were of the most friendly and the decayed industrial life of Italy found a re-birth with the aid of German brains, industry and money. To the same powerful aid Japan owes her present civilisation and greatness. Till the Asquith Government embedded us in a Russian Alliance, Germany longed for and believed in the friendship of England

The Pax Germanica.

The preceding paragraph is frankly pro-German,—with limitations. The best friends of Teutonic culture,—a very real thing,—cannot deny that Prussian militarism had some very hateful aspects. Most armies manage to evolve their Black and Tan elements. Had, however, a wiser foreign policy in Europe generally, and especially in England, given German reformers, who were both powerful and honest, a chance of clipping the wings of the War Party, the present desolation of Europe might have been avoided. It was a real dread of the French *Revanche* and of the Pan-Slavic ambitions of Russia that forced every man of German blood to stake his life and everything he possessed in support of the Kaiser,—whom few Germans admired or respected,—as the emblem of Germanic Nationality and Unity. Precisely a similar state of things, though on a very much smaller scale,

The Panslavist Appears.

presented itself in South Africa a quarter of a century ago. President Kruger did not represent the mass of the Boer people. The vast majority of the young Boers had no affection for the dopper and his dour ways, but the continuous intrigues and threats of Rhodes, Milner, Jameson and the gold magnates forced the pro-English majority, including Botha and Smuts, to stand by their wrong-headed Government in all things. Mr. Chamberlain's claim to "suzerainty" in 1897 was an assault on Boer independence and roused an intense patriotism.

I have shown in the "Pax Germanica" paragraph above that the German Army was actually smaller than that of France alone from 1871 to 1905, but it is urged by the anti-German maniacs that it was so wonderfully trained and drilled and armed that it could trample on and march over all the other armies of the world combined! There never was such a monstrous engine of destruction. All the reliable evidence points to the fact that this masterpiece **The German Army "Old-fashioned" in 1911.** of military genius was in 1911 "old-fashioned," "antiquated" and especially "out of date" in the all-important weapons of artillery. As late as 1912 she was very unprepared for war. Colonel Repington, after witnessing the German manoeuvres, wrote in *The Times*, of which he was military correspondent, on the 28th October, 1911:

"The infantry lacked dash, displayed no knowledge of the use of ground, entrenched themselves badly, were extremely slow in their movements," etc., and "seemed totally unaware of the effect of modern fire." "The cavalry was in many ways exceedingly old-fashioned!" "The artillery, with its out-of-date material (guns) and slow and ineffective methods of fire, appeared so inferior that it can have *no pretension* to measure itself against the French on anything approaching level terms!" And here comes the supreme refutation of the monstrous lies in regard to German militarism: "A nation which after all gives up little more than half its able-bodied sons to the army *has become less militarist than formerly*"!

And this is the fiendish race that Mr. Page, the American Ambassador, assured President Wilson had been preparing for the great war "for forty-five years." The abysmal ignorance of both was equalled only by the sublime stupidity of high-minded and highly educated Englishmen, who seemed to preen themselves on their unparalleled want of knowledge in foreign affairs.

As late as June, 1914, Mr. Ellis Barker, an eminent and extremely anti-German writer, in the *Nineteenth Century*, declared: "*How great the neglect of the German Army has been and how insufficient its strength* can be shown to any layman." He proved that the annual conscription in France was "*50 per cent. larger*" than in Germany, in proportion to the population. That is to say, three French recruits were called to the colours for every two Germans. **"Antiquated Tactics."**

President Kruger (1825-1904), President of the Transvaal Republic 1883-1900. When British miners and capitalists flooded into the Transvaal in search of gold he imposed a 14 year residence qualification for admission to the franchise, and the capitalists were heavily taxed. Lord Milner declared that he was treating free-born Britons as "helots". Britain began to build up its military force in South Africa with a view to enforcing "equal rights". Confronted with this intimidation, Kruger declared war.

O'Donnell's assessment is probably right. Boer politics would have taken a very different course, but for the Boer War, and Kruger's influence on Boer opinion would have been less. He was an utter Scriptural fundamentalist. But that is not the reason why, as late as 1950, people in North West Cork, when they were in high spirits were as likely to shout "Up the Krujer!" as "Up the Rebels!"

The French Army was actually larger in the year before the war than that of Germany, as the French General Buat has since proved. "The German material (chiefly cannon), also, is scarcely up to date," continues Mr. Ellis Barker. "The military outfit of France is superior, according to Lieutenant-Colonel Bézel of the French Artillery and many other experts. The German artillery is inferior to the French. The tactics of the German Army have become antiquated." Marshal Count von Waldersee relates in his *Memoirs* that as early as 1891 "Sir Charles Dilke maintains that the progress made by the French is so enormous that we can no longer claim to be the greatest military power." Dilke had just attended the French manoeuvres as Under-Secretary for War. Soon after his return I met Sir Charles in the House of Commons and nothing could be stronger than his appreciation of the French superiority, without counting the vast preparations of Russia. A memorandum, drawn up by Marshal von Moltke in 1912, denouncing the German civil authorities and the German Parliament for their gross neglect of German military requirements, has recently come to light. The German people up to 1912 resented all militarism and were entirely satisfied with their vast trade, without any warlike adventures and waste of riches and substance.

How different were the facts in England during the six years before 1912. In the first years of the war Mr. Churchill was prominent amongst propagandists in describing "that tiger spring" of Germany, as the then Attorney-General described it, on the unprepared and unsuspecting War Office innocents of Paris, Petersburg, and London. In the middle of 1916 he changed his tune. His bursting vanity and very pardonable pride could not longer conceal from the world the deeds—I am glad to say the very patriotic deeds—of the Master Workmen, Haldane and Churchill. He wrote:

The "Tiger Spring" of which Country?

"Certainly Great Britain's entry into the war was workmanlike. Her large Fleet disappeared into the mist at one end of the island, her small Army hurried out of the country at the other.... It may well be that history furnishes no more remarkable example of the determined adhesion by a Civil Government to the sound principles of war as embodied in carefully considered plans, without regard to the obvious risks and objections."

It should console the average Englishman, alarmed by the myth of unpreparedness, to know that, on the contrary, Great Britain's entry into the war had been so workmanlike, and that both the naval and military activities of the British Government had in 1914, in the accurate words of the First Lord of the Admiralty, "been carefully conceived *in time of peace* and both were in harmony with the highest strategic truth." The conception had been going on for nearly nine years and naturally gave birth to vigorous offspring.

There is still intense bitterness against Germany in many an English home. Men and women do not readily forgive the slayers of their sons and husbands. The accounts of the semi-starvation of prisoners in German camps has added fuel to the fire of hatred. These accounts are very largely true, but they apply chiefly to the latter half of the war.

Demented Mothers.

It is not too much to ask English men and women to give some consideration to the fact that at this period the German people were themselves starving. When the

---

Sir Charles Dilke (1843-1911), a radical Liberal much favoured by Gladstone, who was seen as a future Prime Minister until he was cited as co-respondent in a divorce case.

German Admiral Meurer surrendered his fleet at Scapa Flow in November, 1918, he assigned, as the chief cause of the collapse of his country, the "appalling mortality amongst children" and the hardly less numerous deaths amongst the aged. One of the first Englishmen to enter Berlin after the Armistice, a bitter anti-German, told me himself of the pitiable condition of the working-class men and women, the vast majority of the population. He spoke of the wan, parchment-like faces of all and tottering steps of most. Many American journalists also recorded these facts. There were mad demands from demented mothers for the slaughter of British prisoners. Germany had to feed or half-feed two millions of prisoners, and the most hated of these unhappy men were the British, for the German populace argued that it was their nation that, by the naval blockade, was the whole cause of the shortage of food. Blockade has been said to be the most cruel of atrocities.

At the beginning of the war the feeling towards the British was very different. *Litera scripta manet.* [The written letter remains.] There was a large English colony at Frankfort, and, before leaving on the declaration of war, it sent a letter to the *Frankfurter Zeitung* to say that "as we are about to leave Germany we beg to express our sincerest **"Sincerest Thanks."** thanks to the railway, military, and police officials for the great politeness and prevision, with which they have provided for our journey. In expressing our heartfelt thanks we wish to assure all Germans that, on our part, we shall do our utmost for any Germans, with whom we may be brought in contact in England!" There was no contact, as they were behind wire fences.

The Church of England chaplains of Baden-Baden and Freiburg bore the following testimony "The authorities have exhorted the inhabitants to treat foreigners with respect and courtesy and the people have responded nobly to the appeal. Not only have the hotel and **Three Chaplains.** pension keepers done everything in their power to accommodate their visitors at the most reduced prices, giving credit in many instances, but several cases have come to our notice, in which Germans have nursed and fed English women and children, who were perfect strangers to them, out of pure humanity and good feeling." The chaplain at Berlin writes in August, 1914: "We desire further to affirm that the general attitude towards British subjects *here* has differed very little in friendliness and politeness from their attitude in times of peace." Now, were these reverend clergymen Christian gentlemen or pro-German liars?

These statements were confirmed by many deported Englishmen. A letter in The Times of the 23rd September, from the spokesman of a party of 190, who reached England through Holland, declared that "we received kindness everywhere" in Germany. One of a party from **English Gratitude.** Dantzic tells us that "The Germans have been absolutely

---

the naval blockade. Bomber Harris defended the area bombing of the civilian regions of German cities in 1944/45 by referring to the economic blockade of Germany in 1914-18: "after the last war the British Government issued a White Paper in which it was estimated that our blockade of Germany had caused nearly 800,000 deaths—naturally these were mainly of women and children and old people because at all costs the enemy had to keep his fighting men adequately fed... This was a death-rate much in excess of the ambition of even the most ruthless exponents of air frightfulness." Sir Arthur Harris, **Bomber Offensive**, 1947, p176.

stunning to us!" "We had no lack of money. The Germans were constantly asking us whether we wanted any." English cheques were freely cashed. May I relate a personal episode? My brother, an aged invalid, since deceased, was at this time at the Sanatorium of St. Blasien in the Black Forest and returned to London. His German doctor accepted a cheque of £10 for his fees and the hotel at which he was staying another cheque of that amount for his last week's account. The manager also gladly cashed a cheque for £10 to meet his railway expenses, and just as my brother was driving off to the station he ran after the carriage to press on the invalid another £10, as he feared that the first might be insufficient for a long journey. These four cheques of £10 each have been confiscated by the British Government under a shameful provision of the Treaty of Versailles and two kindly Germans have been mercilessly mulcted. As my brother's executor, I had myself to pay up, out of his estate, to His Majesty's Treasury the £40 due to them!

The question of the British prisoners' camps has not been fairly dealt with. There was much hardship during the middle and end of the war, but even after a year of warfare the Very Rev. Herbert Bury, Church of England Bishop of North and Central Europe, was able to write to *The Times* of the 4th September, 1915, a letter in which he declared that "our chaplain in Berlin, the Rev. H. M. Williams, assures me that in the camps where he has been allowed to go in the way of visiting and ministering, the authorities were ever courteous and helpful and, in his judgment, doing their best to mitigate the hardships of imprisonment for the men." He added, "That is what I hear from other correspondents also, and we have great reason to be grateful to the commandants of the different camps in Germany and in many instances to their wives also." On the 1st September, 1915, the Morning Post published the following statement: "The American Ambassador at Berlin sent to the British Foreign Office two reports by an official of the Embassy, Mr. Jackson, who had visited camps for prisoners of war." One report, on the camp in Westphalia, stated that "it is beautifully situated in a healthy place and is arranged for 10,000 prisoners, housed in barracks which accommodate 500 men each, all being provided with stoves. With all the British prisoners I talked freely, out of hearing of any German, and none had any important complaint to make. The food which I tasted was good. The French cooks told me that the material furnished is good and I saw that the kitchens were clean and well arranged. Meat is provided three times a week. The canteens seemed well stocked and the baths well arranged." I could give other evidence of good treatment before the deadly grip of the British naval blockade brought starvation to all, but none as authoritative as the above from a bishop and an ambassador.

An English Bishop and an American Ambassador.

My brother. Frank Hugh O'Donnell (1848-1916), a Home Rule MP at the time of Isaac Butt, author of **A History Of The Irish Parliamentary Party.** He was fiercely critical of Parnell for facilitating the usurpation by the clergy of the role in public life, and especially in education, which properly belonged to the laity.

The German Fleet And Trade Rivalry
(Chapter XI in original)

The United States In South America

(i) "Britain began this war fully prepared and as if she expected it. Germany was thoroughly unprepared and undoubtedly did not expect war with England."— Mr. A. H. Pollen, at the Mansion House, April, 1915.

(ii) "At the time (June 1914) of the Kiel regatta there was not any intention of going to war on the part of Germany."—Mr. Winston Churchill, December, 1923.

(iii) "Lord Haldane said to me, 'I do not believe that the German Emperor and his advisers really wanted war'."—Very Rev. Dean Inge, January, 1929.

(iv) "July 28th—A note came from Asquith (Secretary of State for War) ordering the 'Precautionary Period' (Semi-mobilisation). This we did. I don't know why we are doing it, *because there is nothing moving in Germany.* We shall see. The Russians have ordered the mobilisation of 16 corps."

"July 30th—Nicholson (Under Secretary, Foreign Office) expects German mobilisation to-morrow."

"July 31st—Eyre Crowe told me that Germany had given Russia 12 hours to demobilise. Russia's answer was an order for 'General Mobilisation'."—Diaries of Field Marshal Sir Henry Wilson, Director of Military Operations, page 153.

How many Englishmen of the present day are aware that it was possible in the second year of the war to make the first of the above statements, yet it was made on the 30th April, 1915, ten months after war began, at the Mansion House in the heart of London, in a lecture by a gentleman, who had long been recognised as a prominent naval authority and expert. It is emphasised by the even more important declaration by Mr. Churchill, a declaration made on oath.

England "Thoroughly Prepared."

The question arises immediately: Was the anti-German agitation by the Asquith Government in 1908-10 in regard to battleships an honest criticism or an extremely unscrupulous political manoeuvre? *The Times* of the 23rd October, 1924, ten years after the War began, at last told the truth and the whole truth. It admitted that the building of dreadnoughts started the whole naval competition, adding:

"Goading their Followers."

"Nobody, however, cared to acknowledge it, and the responsibility for the consequent increase in the British Fleet was ascribed solely to the German armaments. In reality, however, Germany *was building no faster* than the rate laid down in the Naval Law of 1900. The Liberal Cabinet of Mr. Asquith and

---

Dean Inge (1860-1954), Dean of St. Paul's, 1911-34.
Eyre Crowe (1864-1925), influential Foreign Office official, strongly anti-German, author of a 1907 "Memorandum on the present state of Britain's relations with France And Germany". Crowe himself almost fell victim in 1915 to the anti-German frenzy which he had helped to develop. Because he was born in Leipzig, and his mother and his wife were Germans, a press campaign was conducted against him. Crowe survived in office, but Haldane, who had done more than anyone else to prepare Britain for war on Germany, was driven out of office (he was Lord Chancellor), because he had once written favourably about German philosophy.

Sir Edward Grey painted the German danger in the blackest colours, in order to *goad their unwilling followers* to increased sacrifices. It was the year of the Navy Scare, the fleet panic. British newspapers, theatres, cinemas scared the 'man in the street' with the bogy of a German invasion. Sir Edward Grey and other leading politicians overwhelmed the German Ambassador with requests that he should urge the reduction of German naval armaments. Count Wolff-Metternich, a weak man, on his part did not cease to bombard the Kaiser and Chancellor with pessimistic reports."

The Navy Scare was thus, according to *The Times*, a put-up job, intended to mislead the British people, an utterly unscrupulous manoeuvre. "Goading their unwilling followers" by "painting the German danger in the blackest colours" is a very moderate description of those evil days in the House of Commons. I remember them well. How can the British Foreign Office expect ever again to be believed by the statesmen of Europe? The expression *"Perfide Albion"* will have another run of life.

I beg to reproduce on the opposite page two diagrams published in the Statesman's Year Book for 1908, the most reliable, able, and authoritative volume of political statistics in the world. These diagrams in the first and last columns present for the great Naval Powers not only the number of ships in existence in 1908, but those projected up to 1910. The red and green lines in both diagrams show the impassable superiority of the British Navy over that of Germany in battleships of the first and second classes, known in England as Dreadnoughts and King Edwards. So enormous was this superiority that it is apparent to the most casual observer. Not only was there an unapproachable superiority in numbers but, as Mr. Churchill tells in his *World Crisis*, p. 122, "no fewer than twelve ships were actually building on the slips for the Royal Navy, armed with these splendid weapons," the new 13.5 guns, throwing a shell of 1,400 lbs., "quite unsurpassed in the world and firing a projectile nearly half as heavy again as the biggest fired by the German fleet," which was a 1,000- lb shell. Turning to France, the yellow line made clear that, in 1908, she had four Dreadnoughts to one of Germany, and in 1910 would have six to six. In second-class but still very powerful battleships France in 1910 would have thirteen, Russia seven and Germany six. Was not Germany justified in having a naval programme to protect the trade of Dantzic and Memel in the Baltic against Russia and to safeguard against France the far greater commerce of Hamburg and Bremen, facing the Atlantic?

French Superiority at Sea.

Mr. Asquith's camarilla knew, though many members of his Cabinet seemed not to know, that at that time the alliances with France and Russia—alliances is the only truthful word—placed at the disposal of the Allies a battleship strength four times that of Germany. History must come to the conclusion that this agitation was due not to any fear for the fleet of England but for the fleets of France and Russia. If Germany could be frightened into stopping the building of battleships, the two latter Powers would have a great predominance over those of Germany and could destroy her commerce and blockade her coasts. Again and again I protest that I attribute nothing of bad faith to the British people or to the British Parliament, of which I was then a member, but I do allege that there is strong evidence that down to the last pre-war day the British people and the British Parliament were hoodwinked, misinformed, and misled by Mr. Asquith.

Four-fold Strength of Allies.

What extreme justification there was for the German refusal to stop battleship building was brought to light *after the War* by the publication by the Revolutionary Government at Petrograd of many secret political papers. One of these was a

Diagram I

TOTAL NUMBER OF SHIPS IN VARIOUS NAVIES CARRYING GUNS EQUAL OR SUPERIOR TO THOSE OF "DREADNOUGHT" (12 INCH, 45 CAL.)

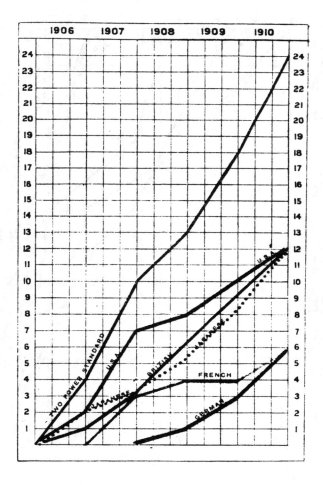

N.B.—In 1917 France had three Dreadnoughts before Germany had one. Diagram II is still more convincing.

Diagram II

TOTAL NUMBER OF SHIPS IN VARIOUS NAVIES CARRYING GUNS EQUAL OR SUPERIOR TO THOSE OF THE "KING EDWARD" CLASS (12 INCH, 40 CALIBRE)

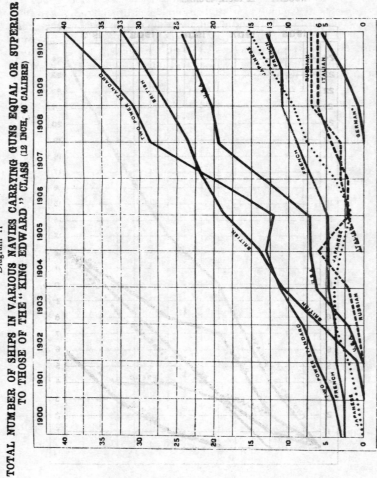

N.B.—in 1910 Germany had the smallest navy of any of the Great Powers.

detailed report, dated the 2nd February, 1911, in which M. Isvolski, the Russian Ambassador in Paris, informed his Chief, M. Sasanoff, the Russian Foreign Minister at Petersburg, that the French Government had adopted a new programme for the French navy, in which provision was made for sixteen new battleships, six new cruisers, twenty destroyers, and fifty submarines! This very, very big programme was actually much larger than the German one of the same period, but it met with no hostile criticism from Mr. Asquith's Admiralty Chiefs or from Sir Edward Grey. How they lied in the House of Commons!

A Very Big Programme.

Far and away the most important revelation came, also after the War, from Grand Admiral von Tirpitz, who, in his book, *Political Documents*, records that when Mr. Haldane, the British War Minister, had his historic conversation with the Kaiser in the Schloss at Berlin, on the 9th February, 1912, "H.M. the Kaiser pointed out that in view of the extended programmes of *our Continental neighbours alone*, we had already been compelled to keep the development of our fleet up to standard. To this Haldane made certain observations to the effect that Great Britain would take care that the French and Russian naval programme would not increase too rapidly. But he refused to go further into *any concrete question* as to the position with regard to France in this matter, since France was laying down three big ships in 1912, while we were considering whether ultimately we would build only two ships."

"France lays down big Ships."

Von Tirpitz alleges that the Haldane proposals, which would probably have led to a peaceful compromise, were wrecked by M. Poincaré, the French President, who refused to accept any limitation of her Navy on the part of France. The day will certainly come when all just men must hold the German people guiltless of any thought of aggressive war. They were forced, as Mr. Lloyd George said on the 1st January, 1914, to struggle for "the very life and independence of the German nation itself."

The Times of the 23rd October, 1924, commenting on these revelations, remarked: "It is *something of a surprise* to find that in the period of 1905-1906 Admiral Tirpitz was against the scheme for increasing the German Fleet, and opposed it with all his power in the interest of maintaining peace with Great Britain. The documents show that in the first phase of the struggle a state of extreme tension arose between the Kaiser and the Chancellor, Prince von Bulow, on the one side, and Admiral von Tirpitz on the other."

Revelations of Admiral von Tirpitz.

In the end, Admiral von Tirpitz proved victorious, though only after sending in his resignation to the Kaiser. He depicts a lively scene, which took place in the Palace in Berlin when the Kaiser realised that he declined to co-operate in accelerating the shipbuilding programme and the slow rate of building, laid down by the Naval Law of 1900, was maintained.

Von Tirpitz resigns.

Not only was the Grand Admiral opposed to any action which might irritate England, but the military chiefs took the same line. *The Times* records that General von Moltke, Chief of the Army Staff, declared that, in his view, war with England must be avoided, and all this time the Liberal Government and its newspapers were working up an intense hatred of Germany for its desire and preparations to destroy the British Navy and the British Empire.

Von Moltke opposes war

The most honourable comment on the naval agitation by Mr. Asquith also appeared in the columns of *The Times*, when its Paris correspondent, Sir Thomas

Barclay, asked very pertinently: "Will the French Navy be free to increase indefinitely while the German Navy is in agreement with us not to do so?... It has obviously become *imperative* for Germany to increase her fleet in proportion to the needs of its protection against an efficient French fleet."

Honourable Comment by The Times

Germany has been much blamed for not accepting the "naval holiday" suggested by Mr. Churchill, but both France and Russia refused to be bound by it. Why was that fact concealed from the British Parliament? Germany was oppressed with terror at the idea of her great trade being destroyed and Hamburg and the Kiel Canal blockaded by a French fleet. It was a far greater danger than any that England could possibly be exposed to.

There cannot be a shadow of a doubt that what chiefly moved English sentiment against Germany was commercial rivalry. The great anti-free-trade organ, the *Morning Post*, on the 25th May, 1916, let the cat out of the bag in this passage:

Commercial Rivalry.

"Before the War this country was sinking into the position of industrial and commercial dependence upon Germany. In the cloth trade we were falling into the position of supplying Germany with yarns and wool, which she worked up into cloth; in the steel trade, the chief source of strength in war, Germany was producing double the output of the United Kingdom. In the smelting of other metals Germany was supreme; in glass and silk we had gone almost out of business; in sugar, which, like cloth, had once been almost a British monopoly, we depended upon Germany. In the electrical trades we maintained a precarious and secondary position. Even upon those industries, in which we seemed to maintain our lead, Germany had a strong hold. Thus our textiles lay at the mercy of German dyes; our confectionery of German sugar; our ship-building relied upon German steel shafting. And in our commerce Germany had as strong a position as in our industry. In banking and on the wool, cotton, leather and stock exchanges the German influence was growing, if not supreme."

British trade "Sinking before the War!" There never was more blatant commercial idiocy or more wilful lying. Before the War British trade was bounding and bursting in its prosperity, chiefly on account of the development of our trade with Germany and the United States. In fifteen years, just the very period of Germany competition, imports and exports practically doubled from £764,558,690 in 1898 to £1,404,151,093 in 1913 (*Statesman's Year Book*). This increase was real, every penny, and in no way influenced by the value of sterling exchange, as might be the case at the present time.

Booming British Trade.

Lord Rothermere, in the *Sunday Pictorial* of a date so late as the 25th November, 1923, stated: "For the last twenty-five years before the War British trade was carried along not by its own momentum but rather by the rapidly increasing prosperity of the world in general." This dictum means, if it means anything, that, so far as Europe was concerned, British trade advanced by the aid of German trade.

The all-important point, however, is that of all the countries of the world Germany was the only one that bought from England nearly as much as she sold to us. In the words of Mr. Harold Cox, the distinguished economist, "Indeed, next to India, Germany was absolutely the best of our pre-War customers." Whilst the United States sent us goods to the value of £141,704,000 in 1913, they bought only £29,297,000. France sold us £46,349,000

Germany our only Big Buyer.

and took only £28,957,000 of British goods. Russia sold us £40,275,000 and bought only £18,116,000 of our manufactures. On the other hand our best customer, Germany, sold us £80,551,000, *but bought £60,573,000 worth of the produce of the British Empire.* In 1906 the figures had been £38,000,000 and £34,000, 000 respectively. By destroying German commerce we cut our own throats. Little wonder that the working men of England, the Labour Party, regard the so-called governing classes of the past, especially the Liberals, as their most stupid advisers.

It is a known fact that very few persons read statistics and still fewer try to understand them,—least of all that purblind and wholly unreliable body, the British Foreign Office. There have not been many more elaborate notes on European politics for a century than the late Sir Eyre Crowe's secret memorandum of January, 1907, on our relations with Germany, and it does not devote a line to our trade with her. So wanting in impartiality was this document that Lord Sanderson, who had been Under-Secretary at the Foreign Office during Lord Salisbury's administration, took the extreme course after his retirement of criticising its misstatements and its anti-German spirit. Sir Eyre Crowe's memorandum was, in fact, an amazingly inaccurate and most vicious attack on German policy, suppressing every fact unfavourable to the policy, which the Foreign Office knew had already been fixed on by the Liberal Imperialist Camarilla. A couple of Lord Sanderson's remarks deserve quotation. They refer to "eventual trade developments in Morocco and China."

A most vicious attack.

"M. Delcassé," he wrote, "ignored Germany entirely when he commenced operations in Morocco." "But in addition there is no doubt that M. Delcasse was steadily pursuing a series of manoeuvres for the purpose of isolating Germany and weakening her alliances." The French attack was directed not only against German trade, but against her political position. Lord Sanderson incidentally referred to the German policy in regard to the Boer War. "Their conduct towards us, though not particularly gracious, was perfectly correct. I see no reason to doubt that Germany declined Mouravieff's invitation to join a European League for the purpose of offering and pressing mediation" in favour of the Boers. The secret despatches published by the Soviet Government since the War prove the loyalty of Germany in this French manoeuvre. "The German Emperor altogether refused any encouragement to President Kruger when he came over to Europe" though he received an ovation from the French Government. During the Boer War "the protests of Germany against our method of exercising the right of search were, no doubt, rude but not altogether without excuse. The almost simultaneous seizure of *three large German mailships,* laden with passengers and cargo, two of which were searched from top to bottom without finding the smallest evidence to justify the step, and the third of which was, no doubt, equally innocent, was an act, which, *if practised on ourselves* would have certainly been denounced as *intolerable.*" These acts were in the opinion of all nations outrages on a friendly power. Can anyone wonder that the United States have definitely said that they will never again put up with such treatment?

Isolating Germany

Seizure of German ships. "Intolerable."

Probably the most dangerous act of the British Foreign Office, one which would have ousted German trade from the richest part of China, is described by Lord Sanderson in these words:

"We had in February, 1898, obtained from the Chinese Government a public engagement that no territory should be

Ousting the German from China.

alienated in the provinces adjoining the Yangtse and the language of the English Press indicated a tendency to regard the valley of that river as the proper sphere of English influence in any partition of interests. The Germans were keen to prevent our acquiring exclusive rights or privileges in this enormous and important tract of country,"—the finest trade area in the Chinese Empire. "The German Emperor told Sir F. Lascelles (our ambassador at Berlin) that he was ready to give us his general support in China, provided we would engage to observe the policy of the open door in the Yangtse Valley. *At that time our relations with Germany were decidedly friendly.*" An agreement was arrived at in October, 1900, which placed on record a community of policy "which the German Government valued, no doubt, mainly on the ground that it kept the Yangtse open to German industrial enterprise." Lord Sanderson added, "I have written these notes because they tend to show that the history of German policy to this country is not the unchequered record of black deeds which the Memorandum (of Sir Eyre Crowe) seems to portray." Indeed, he makes it quite plain that the boot was on the other foot, and that it was France and England which sedulously worked to hamper German commercial activity in world trade. The Continental League formed by Mr. Asquith's Government against Germany and the consequent war were almost entirely due to the clashing of commercial interests.

At the present time it is increasingly manifest that the markets of the South American republics are the object of very far-reaching designs, both in England and the United States. Germany, before the Great War, also had widespread commercial connections, which disappeared completely from the first day of the world conflict. British interests also were wounded almost unto death. America, very naturally, took advantage of the position and developed her business in every field of southern trade, of which she secured practically a monopoly. In 1912 United States investments in the ten largest South American countries were estimated, according to an article in the *Edinburgh Review* of April, 1929, at 174,000,000 dollars, which in last year, 1928, had increased a dozenfold to 2,167,000,000 dollars. After the war almost the first effort of Great Britain was to recover and, if possible, improve her old position. Her most striking manifestation was the visit of the Prince of Wales in 1925 to the southern capitals, and his outspoken call to British commerce. The rival aspirant to trade hegemony soon appeared in the person of Mr. Hoover, who travelled over the same road as soon as his Presidency of the U.S.A. had been assured. England was not slow to counter this exceptional move by the appointment of a special committee of experts, under the chairmanship of Lord D'Abernon, to study South American trade in the republics. It has been singularly successful, having secured £8,000,000 worth of contracts in a couple of weeks. In fact, the race is becoming fast and furious in a manner that cannot fail to get on the nerves of the great commercial and financial combinations involved on both continents. In the past the theory of Admiralty most in favour has been the need of showing the flag on every ocean, because, it is nakedly declared, trade follows the flag. That the British sea-lords firmly believe in this well-founded theory is proved by the whole naval history of England, and it is quite certain that the admirals at Washington have learned the same lesson very thoroughly and with a dangerous rivalry.

In the middle of 1921 we were very near a squabble with the United States about the trade and mines of the Canton Province. Professor Dewey, the distinguished American writer, described in the *New Republic*, of the 6th July, of that year, the very important concessions obtained by a British consortium to the detriment of American interests. "This coal concession is one of the most

Rivalries in South America.

remarkable in all the history of predatory imperialistic finance. It conveys to the British syndicate the right to work the coal of the province, and, after enumerating 22 districts, even, adds to the long list an elastic 'etc.' Further it binds the provincial government to help in expropriating the owners of any prior unworked concession for coal mines. To this monopoly of coal is added what is practically a monopoly of transport, for with it goes it the right to construct any roads, railways, or waterways in the province."

It is to be feared that the commercial exploiter may be in the future, as in the past, the parent of internecine feuds in more than one continent. We must forge a chain to shackle his ubiquitous meddling.

(Chapter XII in original)

What Is Truth?

"The French burnt every town and hamlet through which they passed,
murdering the peasants and outraging the women, totally destroying the
magnificent convent of Alcobaca, the Bishop's Palace at Leiria, and many other
fine buildings, with the mere object of vengeance on the country, to which they
had come as professed friends."—Sir Herbert Maxwell's *Life of Wellington*,
describing the French retreat from the lines of Torres Vedras.

Under the attractive heading of "Lying as a Fine Art" a recent writer in *The
Times* reminds us that: "The Turcomans have a folk-tale concerning a youth, who
escaped execution and won the Khan's daughter as a bride by
telling, one after another, forty incredible lies." I wonder what
would be a becoming reward for the propagandists of Crewe
House. A harem, at least. A few months ago Mr. Rudyard Kipling informed the
students of a Scottish University that to lie was the first use the first man made
of the gift of speech, and who, after the past ten years, will deny the accuracy of
this very Christian gentleman? I fear he was thinking of his own language at
Southampton in June, 1915, when he assured his audience that: "If Germany is
victorious every refinement of outrage which is within the compass of the
German imagination will be inflicted on us in every aspect of our lives." "The
alternative for us is robbery, rape of women, starvation as a prelude to slavery.
That is the *truth*." Dean Inge, of St. Paul's Cathedral, was still more maniacal as
late as the 30th November, 1922, when in the *Evening Standard* he described:

"In *truth* the temper in which Germany began the War. The Germans
meant to conquer the world, and in doing so to perpetrate massacres of non-
combatants on a scale, which would throw the exploits of Attila, Genghiz
Khan and Timour into the shade. The Kaiser and his Ministers would have
been quite unable to keep down the demon, which their systematic poisoning
of the public mind had raised."

"Systematic poisoning of the public mind," also called "truth," is delightful.
I have heard similar truth preached from the altar of the Prince of Peace by the
late Father Bernard Vaughan, whilst the Rev. J. A. Mulry, the President of the
Fordham Catholic University in New York, told a congregation of pious Irish that
when the U.S. Government proclaimed war "it was as though God Himself stood
in my presence and said 'I call you to war.' "

These and other reverend gentlemen may take to heart four simple facts:

(i) The first act of the new French administration of Alsace-Lorraine was to
evict the Crucifix of Christ from the public schools, where the Germans held it
in honour.

(ii) The French military authorities, in invading German territory, have forced
the Municipal authorities of the Catholic Rhineland,—the best Catholics in the
world, "the most docile, the most hard working and the most intelligent people
in Europe," as General Smuts described them,—to provide brothels for their
Negro African troops. Mr. Norman Angel has described this abomination in the
Contemporary Review of September, 1926.

(iii) When some twenty years ago the infidel Government of France confiscated all Catholic Churches and buildings, the Paris *Figaro* reported that the communist municipality of Vendome had gone one better by converting a Catholic Church and its grave-yard into a public latrine.

(iv) Cardinal Logue, the Archbishop of Armagh, stated in October, 1914, that: "He did not believe there was any use in having Catholic chaplains in hospitals in France. He saw a formula to be signed by any soldier before he could have a priest in these hospitals. This formula and the requirements of this condition were devised from the beginning to deprive dying Catholic soldiers of any chance of receiving the Sacraments."

I speak with feeling as a Catholic and an Irishman. He knows little of the history of the sixteenth century who is unaware that the success of the Reformation was chiefly due to a shameless propaganda that represented every priest and nun as at best disreputable. The chapters in   "The Dean Maitland's *Dark Ages*, entitled "The Ribalds," give a   Ribalds." few examples of the unclean charges made. As a young man I travelled much in Europe, and everywhere came up against the lies and scurrilities of the enemies of Ireland.

I will now attempt to appreciate a few of the charges laid against the German armies and people in the early days of the War. The blood-curdling report of the British Commission, under the chairmanship of Lord Bryce, refers entirely to this short period. During this time the   "Professional German military authorities were particularly anxious to   and Personal conciliate American opinion, and the correspondents of   Word and American journals were allowed to move about the war area   Honour." with extraordinary freedom. After about two months of war four American correspondents, Mr. Roger Lewis, of the Associated Press; Mr. Irvin S. Cobb, of the *New York Evening Post*; Mr. Henry Hanson, of the *Chicago Daily News*; and Mr. James Bennett, of the *Chicago Tribune*, horrified at the monstrous charges made, issued a joint memorandum,—it is too long to quote in full,—in which they pledged their "professional" and "personal" word and honour that after many weeks with the German Army in Belgium they had not seen "a single instance" of atrocity. "So far as we have seen there has been no mistreatment of civilians by soldiers." Mr. Irvin Cobb subsequently added: "Every one of the refugees had a tale to tell of German atrocities on non-combatants, but *not once* did we find an avowed eye-witness to such things. Always our informant had heard of the torturing or maiming or the murdering, but never had he personally seen it. It had always happened in another town." "Though sundry hundreds of thousands of German soldiers had gone this way no burnt houses marked their wake." These American gentlemen may have been modern Ananiases, but there is nothing *a priori* to suggest that they were liars. Even the special correspondent of the *Daily Mail*, writing from Rouen in the first week of September, 1914, stated: "Certainly panic in Normandy seems wholly unwarranted. I feel bound to mention the report of M. Goubet, Councillor-General of the Pas de Calais, who arrived here last night, in regard to alleged Uhlan atrocities in the north of France. M. Goubet declares emphatically: "I have witnessed nothing like what has been reported from Belgium. The enemy progresses, doing no injury to the inhabitants beyond occasionally damaging property where hospitality is refused. *They pay for all food.*' " and everything else.

There never was a war since the beginning of recorded time, which did not reek of atrocities, big and little. War is war, and war is hell. In   "A Blackened regard to burning and devastation in war, no European nation   Wilderness." has a cleaner record than England, yet a gentleman, who is now a Cabinet Minister, in *The Times History of the Transvaal War*, vol. v, pp. 158-65, and 254, wrote of Lord Kitchener's scheme of universal devastation and depopulation," "organised pillage and destruction," "wholesale destruction and slaughter of cattle, sheep and horses." "A blackened wilderness,"—not to mention mal-administered concentration camps, with 20,000 child victims. In America, Sherman's devastation of the Carolinas and Sheridan's of the Shenandoah Valley in 1865, were both more thorough and pitiless than in South Africa. Nothing that Germany did in Belgium and France was one-tenth part as terrible or systematic. "Military necessity," which we scoff at in German mouths, is, unfortunately, a very real thing. *Salus civitatis suprema lex.* British national

Copenhagen. security in 1807 necessitated our taking action to prevent the Danish fleet falling into the hands of our powerful French enemy, and to enforce our demand we were compelled to bombard Copenhagen, the capital of a neutral nation, at peace with us, causing great loss of civilian lives and buildings.

The Germans have issued a big report describing the atrocities committed on them by the Belgians. It, however, admits that many hundreds of Belgian

"They were Shot. civilians, mostly *francs-tireurs*, were shot by drum-head courts-martial. It was a hideous total, but the German armies were fighting for their lives. It is the essence of war that you are justified in killing every man who is trying to kill you, attacking from in front. What about attacking in the back? All honour to every man or woman who tries to destroy the invaders of the motherland, but they must take the dread consequences. The Italians did exactly the same thing as the Germans. Soon after they entered the war, Reuter's Agency reported: "In the Tolmino and Friuli the Austrians have organised bodies of *francs-tireurs*. About 100 of these were caught red-handed with, besides arms, a large amount of Austrian money in their possession, for which they were unable to account. *They were shot.* This severe example, the evacuation of some villages and the manifestoes issued by the authorities threatening capital punishment for such offences have cleared the district." Lord Roberts gave short drift to the Boer horsemen who cut the railway in the rear of his advancing troops. Guerilla warfare knows no mercy and gives no quarter. The London *Standard* printed a Pretoria Dispatch dated 9th August 1900, which stated that "The Boers sniped a train at Bronkhurst yesterday on the line between Pretoria and Middleburg. Two of its occupants were wounded. In accordance with Lord Roberts's warning all the farms were fired within a radius of ten miles."

Very few writers on the earliest days of the War recognise how great was the service rendered by these brave Belgian civilian-soldiers, often led by their priests,

No Battle of the Marne. as in Spain during Napoleon's invasion. By all the laws of war the Germans were justified in shooting them when taken prisoner, for they were one of the chief causes of the German disaster on the Marne. The delay of food and munitions from Germany on the Belgian railways, due to their patriotic *sabotage*, rendered further German advance impossible. After the German retreat hundreds of German soldiers were found dead of starvation, their mouths red from the raw beetroot, which was the only food they could find. Indeed there was no Battle of the Marne, in the proper sense of battle, but a severe punishment of the German troops as they hurriedly retired.*

---

* Marshal Foch in his *Memoirs* published in the beginning of 1931, definitely states that "signs of a precipitate retreat abounded." In addressing his troops on the 8th September, 1914, he told them that the German Army had ceased to exist as an army. "Having been

[to page 77.]

Field-Marshal Lord French, in his "1914," pp. 114-19, writes that before the battle "It was impossible for me to know the situation accurately in all its details. For instance, I could not then know, as I know now, that the Germans had abandoned their vigorous offensive twenty-four hours earlier than this, nor should I have conceived it possible." Naturally, inasmuch as it was not due to military failure or defeat. "I did not know at that time that a retreat had really set in." "In action early in the day,"—the first day of the British advance,—"it was discovered that a general retreat was in progress, covered by rearguards. On this I gave orders that the enemy was to be closely pressed." There was no battle on the Marne with the mass of the German Army, but a vigorous assault on its retreating rearguards. And that is an end of many French heroics, of General Manoury and his Paris taxi-cabs. The mortality was on both sides relatively small. "Our casualties were slight," writes Lord French.

As to the material devastation of Belgium, we now learn from no less an authority than the late Lord Northcliffe that there was gross exaggeration. Writing in *The Times* of June, 1922, he stated: "There is an inclination in the mind of the public to exaggerate the amount of damage done to Belgium by the Germans.... The German Army lived in Belgium for years, spent money there and I say without hesitation that Belgium is the most prosperous country I have seen since I left New Zealand." No wonder. The Germans paid freely for everything they needed after the Belgian *francs-tireurs* stopped sniping at German soldiers by day and tearing up the railways by night. Many villages were shell-torn and burnt out, but the total damage was undoubtedly small considering the mighty war and vast armies that swept across her face.

"The Most Prosperous Country."

After two and a half years of the German occupation of Belgium, that is, practically in the middle of the War, *The Times* of the 31st March, 1917, gave prominence to a vivid and "amazing picture" of Belgium, as seen by one of its correspondents, a Mr. J. P. Whitaker. After a tour through the villages between Brussels and Antwerp he found "no scarcity of good food." "Meat was plentiful, especially home-bred pork." So well fed was this gentleman that "I actually found myself gaining in flesh." "The Germans refrain from commandeering the Belgian supplies of food." "The natives are allowed to travel by railway without hindrance." "The policy of the Germans, in short, appears to be to interfere as little as possible with the everyday life of the country. The fruits of this policy are seen in a remarkable degree in Brussels. All day long the main streets of the city are full of bustle and all the outward manifestations of prosperity. Women in short fashionable skirts, with high-topped fancy boots, stroll completely at their ease along the pavement, studying the smart things, with which the drapers' shop windows are dressed. Jewellers' shops, provision stores, tobacconists and the rest show every sign of 'business as usual.' Even the sweetstuff shops had well-stocked windows. The theatres, music-halls, cinema palaces and cafes of Brussels were open and crowded." It seems to have been not half a bad thing to live in "tortured" Belgium under the Hun-Boche war administration.

"An Amazing Picture."

---

in movement without halt since the opening of the campaign," Marshal Foch declared that "the German Army has reached the extreme limit of its endurance. In most of the units (battalions) officers and non-commissioned officers *no longer exist*. Regiments are marching mixed up together and general officers *have lost control*." Without food and without ammunition they could offer little resistance to the fresh French troops brought from Paris by Generals Manoury and Gallieni. [Note by O'Donnell.]

The Germans acted in Belgium as they did in France in 1871-3. Marshal MacMahon, President of the French Republic, in a letter, dated the 4th September, 1873, to General Manteuffel, commanding the German army of occupation, wrote: "I deem it my duty to express to its Commander-in-Chief the sentiments which I experience on account of the justice and impartiality shown by him in the difficult mission which was entrusted to him."

"Justice and Impartiality."

How have French and Belgian officials and generals acted in the Ruhr towards hapless German men and women in times of peace?

Louvain must be separately dealt with. Its ruined University, dear to every Irishman, is a horrible monument to the God of War. We have a clear statement of what occurred from a special correspondent of the *Daily Mail*, on 3rd September, 1914, Mr. A. J. Dawe, who was in the German lines from Brussels to Aix-la-Chapelle in disguise. "There can, of course, be no doubt that Louvain offered considerable resistance. The civic population, led by the Mayor and Belgian officers, worked machine guns upon the German trains as they approached the station, and the Church of St. Pierre, which overlooks the station, was turned into a veritable fort. The civilists fired upon the incoming troop trains from the windows and from behind the buttresses."

"A Veritable Fort."

On the same day, 3rd September, on which the *Daily Mail* published Mr. Dawe's account, a distinguished war correspondent, Mr. Gerald Morgan, corroborated its facts in the *Daily Telegraph* in the course of a description of how nearly Brussels escaped from the consequences of a similar insurrection against the Germans by the civilian population. An eminent American writer, Mr. Richard Harding Davis, accompanied Mr. Morgan and honestly described the civilian warfare in American journals.

As a matter of fact, some German troops had been repulsed at Malines and had fallen back on Louvain in disorder. The citizens thought that the time had come to strike a patriotic blow for their country,—all honour to them. None were more brave than the students of the University, the buildings of which had become the centre of the rising, where also the last glorious stand was made. Many houses were burned in the street fighting.

"The Last Stand."

The invasion of Eastern Prussia in the first week of war by the Russian armies was a real devastation like the Transvaal or the Shenandoah Valley. Mr. Belloc, without a word of condemnation, estimated that the damage amounted in value to £20,000,000. The large town of Memel, bigger than Louvain, was burned to the ground, and the *Morning Post* gave its joyous approval in these words: "We are heartily glad that the Russians burned Memel and we hope that the Allies will burn a good many more German towns before this war is over." On the 23rd September, 1914, the London *Times* published a long account from its war correspondent describing "the wholesale looting" of the German towns by the Russian soldiery. "Large towns have been completely sacked. The streets are covered with broken furniture, glass, and china from the plundered houses. The Cossacks smash everything portable or detachable. They cover the roads with fragments of furniture, curtains, rugs, gramophones, inches deep." At the same time Reuter's telegrams recounted that "the Poles, Ruthenians and Jews, inhabiting the districts invaded by Russia, have already, some 70,000 of them, sought refuge in Vienna from the atrocities of the Russian soldiery." *The Times* made no mention in its leading articles of these evidences of Russian civilisation. Only Germany gives birth to Huns! War is war, and war is hell.

"Large Towns completely Sacked."

The world was horrified early in September, 1914, by this official statement of the French Government:

"Without being able to plead military exigencies, and solely for the pleasure of destruction, the German troops have subjected Rheims Cathedral to a systematic and furious bombardment." **Rheims, an Official Lie.**

Knowing what half a dozen shells would do, if there was any real intention to destroy a relatively fragile building like a church, the Press of Europe and America quite naturally assumed that the ancient and beautiful Cathedral had been levelled with the ground and burst unto a wild cry of execration against the criminals who could be guilty of such an enormity. The lie got a splendid start and, though educated men soon learned the truth, you can still hear of this awful sacrilege of the German, Hun, and Vandal at ladies' tea parties in London and Washington.

The Cathedral was not injured by shell-fire but, in the words of a French officer, quoted in the London *Globe* of 22nd September, 1914, "at 2 p.m. on Sunday the Cathedral was badly damaged inside where some straw caught fire. Woodwork in the interior has been destroyed, but the Cathedral itself is not beyond repairing." The Paris correspondent of *The Times*, telegraphing on the 20th September, admitted that the German bombardment "appears to have been provoked"—by the fact that the "French planted their artillery in the city itself and replied to the enemy's guns with great vigour." There were several batteries in the great square in front of the Cathedral. **Straw Fire not Shell-fire.**

The *Westminster Gazette* of the 13th November, 1915, confirmed the above statements in the words: "The Cathedral is not beyond repair. The outer wooden roof, which was needed to protect the stone roof from the weather, has been burned, but the Cathedral looks better without this ugly hump on its back. The stone roof, except for a small hole, is entirely as it was. A new roof will probably be made of slate and asbestos. Half of the celebrated orange window is broken, but much glass has been saved wherewith to repair it. *The two organs are untouched, as are the paintings, the pulpits, and the chapels;* and the Cardinal goes very often to pray in his private chapel. It was the burning of the straw, on which German wounded were lying, that was responsible for so much damage to the interior."

Writing as an eye-witness, Mr. Ward Price narrated in the *Daily Mail* of 21st September, how "the Abbe Andrieux, one of the Canons of the Cathedral, and M. Guedet took me up the winding staircase in the thick walls to the top of the high Cathedral tower and I got a clear idea of the battle." "The Cathedral tower was a wonderful grand stand **A Wonderful Grand Stand.** from which to watch this appalling game of destruction." The Germans fired shrapnel several times at the tower to clear out the French officers, *who were directing* the French Artillery by their observations." Mr. Ward Price added that, "one can hardly imagine that the German gunners could miss so huge a mass as Rheims Cathedral, towering as it did above the town, if they had really wished to reach it." The immunity of the great church is, no doubt, connected with the fact that the German soldiers were South German corps, all Catholics, under the command of the Catholic Duke Albrecht of Wurtemburg. With a truthfulness that befits a great churchman, Cardinal Lucon, Archbishop of Rheims, in a letter to the *Echo de Paris*, dated the 27th September, 1914, stated that "the walls of the edifice and the great organ are intact." **Walls Intact**

The last "atrocity" that I would ask my readers to consider is the alleged misuse of submarines in the destruction of mercantile ships. As I am not an expert in such matters I leave it to those who ought to know what they are writing about. A

"Perfectly in Order." fortnight before the War, Admiral Sir Percy Scott, in reply to some remarks by Lord Sydenham, considered the question fully in a letter in *The Times* of the 16th July, 1914. He first quoted the opinion of a foreign naval officer of "high experience," apparently French, on the law of submarine blockade to the following effect:

"If we went to war with an insular country, depending for its food on supplies from overseas, it would be our business to stop that supply. On the declaration of war we should notify the enemy that she should warn those of her merchant ships coming home not to approach the island, as we were establishing a blockade of mines and submarines. Similarly we should notify all neutrals that such a blockade had been established, and that if any of their vessels approached the island they would be liable to destruction either by mines or submarines, and therefore would do so at their own risk."

This is exactly what the Germans did. Sir Percy Scott agreed absolutely with this opinion and proceeded:

"Such a proclamation would, in my opinion, be *perfectly in order*, and once it had been made if any British or neutral ships disregarded it they could not be held to be engaged in the peaceful avocations referred to by Lord Sydenham, and if they were sunk in the attempt, it could not be described as a relapse into savagery or piracy in its blackest form. If Lord Sydenham will look up the accounts of what usually happened to the blockade-runners into Charleston during the Civil War in America, I think he will find that the blockading cruisers seldom had any scruples about firing into the vessels they were chasing or driving them ashore, and even peppering them when stranded with grape and shell. The mine and the submarine torpedo will be newer deterrents."

American Example.

Infinitely more important, however, are the statements of Admiral Lord Fisher made in a special article in *The Times* of the 26th November, 1919, a year *after the War* had ended, which afterwards were reproduced by him in a book, entitled *Records*. He lays down the principle that, "the essence of war is violence and that moderation in war is imbecility." Von Tirpitz could not be more plain spoken. He developed his arguments in regard to "Submarines and Commerce" in these words:

"She Must Sink Her Captures."

"Again, the question arises as to what a submarine can do against a merchant ship when she has found her. She cannot capture the merchant ship; she has no spare hands to put a prize crew on board. Harmless trader in appearance, in reality she may be one of the numerous fleet auxiliaries, a mine-layer, or carrying troops, and so on." Field-Marshal Lord Grenfell in his *Memoirs*, published in the *Morning Post* on the 23rd October, 1926, condemning an official report published in India, remarked: "To publish such a report in the middle of a great war was the greatest possible political mistake, and the Germans got much valuable information out of it, especially the fact that ammunition was carried in what are called Hospital Ships, the real fact being that wounded soldiers, supplies, and ammunition were all forwarded together. Hospital ships were apparently not properly organised till after the War Office had taken over the direction of the campaign. It was a lamentable case of dirty linen being washed in public." "The apparent merchant ship," continued Lord Fisher, "may also be armed. In this light, indeed, the recent arming of our British merchantmen is unfortunate, for it gives the hostile submarine an excellent excuse (if she needs one) for sinking them,—namely, that of self-defence against the guns of the merchant ship. What can be the answer to all the foregoing but that (barbarous and inhuman as, we again repeat, it may appear), if the submarine is used at all against commerce, *she must sink her captures?*"

"She must sink her captures." War is war, and war is hell. All war is barbarous and inhuman. "Moderation in war is imbecility." Infinitely the most inhuman act of war is the blockade, which avowedly is not aimed at soldiers or sailors, but at the aged and the child, the babe and the woman. In the Middle Ages the Catholic Church inflicted the major excommunication on any general who blockaded a town before he had given full opportunity for the withdrawal of women and children. In those uncivilised days there was such a thing as "The Truce of God."

Pope Benedict XV, in condemning the sinking of the *Lusitania*, said; "I know no more frightful crime. How distressing to see our generation a prey to such horror! But do you think the blockade which hems two Empires and condemns millions of innocents to famine is prompted by very humane sentiments?"

A further question arises as to whether the German submarines carried out their odious duties in an especially "inhuman" manner. So strong, so explicit were the allegations that I, like every Briton, believed that the charge was only too true. During my recent visit to the United States I quite accidentally **"Legitimate** picked up a monthly review for June, 1923, called *Current* **and Humane."** *History*, published by the New York Times Company, and noticed that the first article was entitled "Rear-Admiral Sims on U-Boat Atrocities, Champions Submarines." I knew Admiral Sims to be as pro-British as the whole of the Pilgrims' Club rolled together, the nearest approach to a full-blooded John Bull that the United States could produce. Two of the first sentences of this striking article declared that, in condemning submarine warfare, "The United States are deprived by the Naval Treaty (of Washington) of a *legitimate and humane* method of destroying an enemy's commerce," and that, "one of the aims of this article is to correct the impression that all German naval officers were habitually guilty of acts of savage cruelty."

The evidence of Admiral Sims is peculiarly valuable in regard to submarines, as it was his special duty on arriving in England to devise measures, in co-operation with Admiral Jellicoe, to defeat their "terribly destructive" operations. I make a few quotations from this article:

(i) "War-stimulated hatred has created the belief that the common practice of the German submarine commanders was not only simply to murder the crews of the merchant ships torpedoed, but to do so with all the savage cruelty they could conceive of. There were attributed to these officers by honest people many atrocities of such an inhuman and revolting nature, that in normal times one would consider them beyond the possibility of belief by any persons not still suffering from war monomania. I have met many such people who, though normally thoughtful and kindly Christians, honestly believe these *awful yarns*.

(ii) "Ever since my return from the War in April, 1919, I have tried to make the significance of the submarine clear to our people. I have explained it in untechnical terms to more than *one hundred audiences*, also in a popular account in a book of several hundred pages and in a number of articles, but apparently without much success in making it really understood. *The* **The Press** *Press has appeared to be unwilling to publish the facts*." **Conceals**

(iii) "Within the past few months, in speaking to various **the Truth.** audiences on the operations of the German submarines, I have stated that their commanders were specially selected and thoroughly trained men, and that most of the accounts of atrocities popularly attributed to them were untrue. The submarine commanders generally acted in a humane manner in carrying out the orders of their Government, in some instances giving the boats of torpedoed merchant vessels *food and water* and a tow toward land, and sending out wireless signals giving their position."

It took many years before the American Press published these well-authenticated facts.

[Miscellaneous Chapter]

Mr. Asquith seemed to me to be intellectually anti-Irish, anti-Catholic, and, I am inclined to think, anti-Labour, though the exigencies of his politics drove him in the opposite directions. He had for years been living in the degenerate atmosphere of "The Souls"* and in it lost his own political soul. His ambition seemed to be to conciliate Conservative opinion... I am far from blaming the strong Conservative tendencies in his character, quite the other way, but he was entirely incapable of evolving a measure of self-government that would satisfy an Irish Nationalist.

*The following description of one of the best of them, a brave and brilliant young man, under the semi-pagan influence of the "Souls", makes painful reading: "Raymond Asquith—killed in battle 14th September, 1916—was intellectually one of the most distinguished young men of his day and beautiful to look at, added to which he was light in hand, brilliant in answer, and interested in affairs. When he went to Balliol he cultivated a kind of cynicism which was an endless source of delight to the young people around him; in a good-humoured way he made a butt of God and smiled at man."— **Autobiography of Margot Asquith**.

And this is our *Kultur*.

[The Irish Future, p19]

[Raymond Asquith was the Prime Minister's son by his first wife. Margot Tennent, who became Asquith's second wife, was a member of the Souls in the early 1890s, before her marriage, and continued to be so after. The souls were a group specialising in brilliant conversation on art and politics and things in general. They fit in between the Pre-Raphaelites and the Bloomsbury Group, but were considerably less earnest than either. However, their centrepiece was A.J. Balfour, who was certainly the last philosopher/Prime Minister of Britain, and perhaps the only one. Though Balfour was very doubtful about progress, he decided when he was Irish Secretary that it would be a good thing if the peasants replaced the landlords as the owners of the land, and the 1903 Land Act was implemented when he became Prime Minister. Balfour was a languid aristocrat. Asquith, though he cultivated a patrician manner, was an upstart from a Yorkshire Scriptural fundamentalist family of tradesmen. He would have been out of his element among the Souls, but he participated in such things vicariously through Margot. B.C.]

It is the want of education that has often placed Irish politicians in an undesirable position. At the beginning of the Great War they were the victims of anti-German propaganda, of fables which were believed, no matter how absurd. Thus Mr. Redmond thundered against the German soldiery, very largely Catholic, telling the people of Waterford in December 1914, that "the Boches were hunting priests and nuns and wantonly destroying Catholic Churches". He never learned, I dare say, that in an interview granted in 1915 to M. Latapie, the correspondent of the Paris **Liberte**, Pope Benedict XV stated in regard to the charge of ill-usage of priests in Belgium, a very favourite falsehood in Catholic countries, that "the

Cardinal Secretary has received reports from seven Belgian congregations", Dominicans, Jesuits, Franciscans, and others, "that they had not a single case to bring forward."

[The Irish Future p23]

It would be a long story indeed to tell how the Home Rule of Isaac Butt sickened in the hands of the incompetent Parnell and the Socialist Davitt, and how it died in those of the kindly John Redmond. Under the former it was practically displaced by the Land League and its anarchist war on wealthy Irishmen. Under the latter Home Rule was an inert survival and little but a name. For four years in the House of Commons, 1906-1910, I watched, as a London member, its quiet disintegration and its impotent old age before its death in the short Easter Rebellion of 1916. I do not think that the Irish members knew of the anger with which they were regarded by Nationalist Irish, whilst a good-humoured disregard of them and of all their wishes was their lot in Parliament. Except for occasional outbursts from John Dillon and Joe Devlin, no Nationalist movement in any assembly was ever supported by such meek and mild representation. They had their field days and much eloquence was wasted on empty benches, but the Liberal Whip could usually rely on Irish subservience…

The Irish Party may, indeed, be said to have ceased to be a political force in 1905 with the advent of the Liberal Party to office under the Premiership of Sir Henry Campbell-Bannermann, who had given a shameful pledge to he Liberal Imperialists, under Mr. Asquith, to drop the Home Rule policy, immediately after having secured the large Irish vote throughout England and Scotland by the warmest advocacy of the Irish cause. Yea, politics are an unclean thing.

[The Irish Future, p59/61]

[The 1912 Home Rule Bill came about because the Liberals lost their overall majority in 1910 and were dependent on the Irish Party to form a Government.]

I am glad to say that my brother, Mr. Frank Hugh O'Donnell, withdrew from this contaminated party in 1884.

[ibid p66]

[T. P. O'Connor's service to Britain among the American Irish during the War: see Introduction, p46.]

Mr. Winston Churchill's **Aftermath**, in many ways a singularly honest book, recognises the folly and wickedness of Lord Kitchener's policy, but tries to excuse it solely by reference to the civil rebellion of 1798, over a century ago. Irishmen are blamed for their long memories of ancient grievances and Cromwellian devilries, but the War Office in 1914 had absolutely no justification for its vindictive reminiscences. Its action was rank Orangeism and Toryism of the most hateful kind.

[The Irish Future p95]

In the ordinary Englishman's mind the history of Europe seems to have begun in 1871, that is, at the end of the Franco-German War, when the infamous conquerors despoiled their gentle neighbour of the rich French provinces of Alsace and Lorraine, clearly an act particularly wicked and brutal. How many Englishmen know or remember how these provinces became part of France?

[The Irish Future, p137/8]

There have been few more misleading propaganda (sic) than the outcry regarding devastation in France and Belgium. It was wonderfully small, except when caused by artillery fire. Millions and millions of shells and other explosives played havoc and levelled the houses of many towns and villages, but of wanton destruction there was extremely little.

A summary of modern European history would show that since the beginning of the 17th century French armies have twice crossed the Pyrenees to attack Spain. Six times have they crossed the Alps to attack Italy. Nine times have they crossed the Danube to attack Austria. It is hard to say how often they have crossed the Rhine to ravage Germany.

[The Irish Future, p143/4]

Patriotic lying has been the bedrock of European politics for a decade or more. Lie-bred hatred was at the root of the recent war, so far as the British Empire was concerned. This is true also of the United States. Fortunately, outside the evil ranks of professional politicians, there is a mass of straight men and women who love the truth for its own sake and seek it. They are, however, generally ill-acquainted with the intricacies of foreign politics and have been grievously misled by ignorant or mischievous advisers."

[The Lordship Of The World. Introduction to the Third Thousand. p5]

Conservatives deplore the decay of British influence in Europe, but they should remember that they themselves abandoned the wise foreign policy of Lord Salisbury, which favoured Germany, and, with a stupid intensity, backed the war policy of Mr. Asquith, which has resulted:

(i) In the destruction of three great centres of Continental Conservatism at Vienna, Berlin and Petersburg;

(ii) In setting up a dozen republics and letting loose the forces of Communism in half the countries of Europe, and

(iii) In the diminution of British authority in India, Egypt and Ireland, not to mention the manifold injuries to our trade. That is what betrayed England owes to the secret and unauthorized diplomacy of Sir Edward Grey, as described by the Earl of Birkenhead and Mr. Winston Churchill, two of the most observant minds among British statesmen. Sir Edward Grey was also the most anti-Irish member of Mr. Asquith's Cabinet. He is now naturally a protagonist of Orange unreason, the "one bright spot", according to Lord Carson, in the British firmament. He and the now Earl of Oxford and Asquith—an absurd title—put all England's money on a short war, "over by Christmas", and lost most of it.

[Lordship Of The World p15-16]

At the time the war broke out I had been for a couple of years the official Liberal candidate for the Northern Division of Hampshire, which included the great military headquarters of Aldershot, and had ample opportunity of witnessing the loyal enthusiasm not only of the regular Irish Regiments, like the Munsters, Connaughts and Dublin Fusiliers, but of "Redmond's Army", who were encamped to the number of 10,000 within a few miles from our home at Eversley. I spoke on many recruiting platforms, but soon came to know that things were going badly for Irishmen.

[Lordship Of The World p133-4]

Can even Conservatives wonder that Englishmen are turning to Labour in the hope that they may find 'men who will not lie'. In his World Crisis... Mr.

Churchill lays stress on the shady, double-faced conduct he admires. "Sir Henry Campbell-Bannermann was still receiving the resounding acclamations of Liberals, peace lovers, anti-jingoes and anti-militarists in every part of the country" when he authorized Sir Edward Grey to secretly grope his way up the backstairs of the French Foreign Office. If there is a shadow of truth in the belief that the British nation is a democracy, no language can be too strong to condemn such a policy, for it is now freely admitted that if Grey had plainly and openly told Germany what England's intentions were, we never would have had the murderous war of 1914-18. Indeed, the German people were as successfully misled as the English. Mr. Churchill, giving evidence in his civil suit against Lord Alfred Douglas on the 11th December, 1923, stated: "I do not think that at the time of the Kiel Regatta (June 1914) there was any intention of going to war *on the part of Germany*, but the whole situation was altered by the murder of the Archduke". The right honourable gentleman was then on his oath. One would like to have Mr. Asquith and Lord Haldane in the witness box of a High Court of Justice.

It is, however, necessary and just to recognise that the Liberal Imperialists were in a sense honest and, in their short-sighted folly, patriotic. They were carrying out—secretly and shamefacedly—the old British policy of the Balance of Power...

This is a war policy, a policy of attack and not defence, of diplomatic and international combinations to humble every powerful European nation. It worked admirably against Louis XIV and the Great Napoleon, but in those days there was no **tertius gaudens**, like the United States, to supplant our trade, whilst Britain poured out her blood and her treasure. It is a policy that needs a long head, which the inexperienced, stolid Sir Edward Grey did not possess.

[The Lordship Of The World p12]

Nemesis: Casement & Connolly
"Every nation, if it is to survive as a nation, must study
its own history and have a foreign policy"
(C.J. O'Donnell, The Lordship Of The World, 1924, p145).

Independent Ireland has never had what could rightly be called a foreign policy, and for the past quarter century it has not studied its own history. And, by consequence, its existence has become problematical to itself. This was particularly noticeable in 1991, the 75th anniversary of the Easter Rising. The 50th anniversary had been extensively commemorated. And, as I recall it, it was commemorated in Britain hardly less than in Ireland. I was living in London at the time, and was there subjected to a great outpouring of stage-Irishism—which was a new thing to me because I had never experienced it in Slieve Luacra. It seems in retrospect that 1966 was a year of great illusion. There was the illusion that Lemass had made a progressive overture towards the North. And there was the illusion that the Easter Rising had been taken on board by British culture.

But the Easter Rising was not a West British event, and British culture has long since lost the imaginative power which might have made it such after the event.

The independent Irish state originated in the Great War on the anti-British side. But nationalist Ireland never produced directly out of its own culture a single history of that war. That monumental oversight is at the source of the embarrassment which was so widely felt on the 75th anniversary of the Rising.

Something of the flavour of the actual event still survived in 1966, because many of those who had taken part in the Rising or the War of Independence still survived and were held in some esteem. But, between the 50th and the 75th anniversaries, they died off, and the intellectuals who had developed under their influence had their memories erased and their values devalued when Vatican 2 began to exert its disorientating influence on society from 1970 onwards.

Between the 50th and the 75th anniversaries, journalists, historians, and politicians have systematically stripped the Rising of all actual context. And, having thus deprived it of a great part of its character and reduced it to an isolated event—a gratuitous act of violence—they naturally find it barren.

Ireland has no foreign policy. While the affairs of the world were locked up in the feud between the two great military powers which won the 1941-45 war, neutrality passed muster (in "Albert R.N." fashion) as a foreign policy though it was actually an evasion of policy. But now that the Cold War is over and done with, and the world no longer consists of two great armies between which one can strike a pose of virtuous neutrality, the semblance of policy which once attached to neutrality has blown away. Neutrality can now express nothing but what O'Donnell called "meanness of ideal" (ibid).

In human affairs there is no absolute existence, only relationships. Peoples, like individuals, delineate themselves through interaction with others. Even the Chinese Empire, the most smug and self-sufficient major civilisation the world has seen, related to the rest of the world, even if only by seeing it as barbarian.

A nation-state relates to the world, and gives definition to itself, by its foreign policy. Lacking a foreign policy, Ireland is incomplete as a state. And yet the independent Irish state proclaimed in 1916 had its first beginning in foreign policy.

The change from Home Rule Ireland to independent Ireland begins in August 1914 in the sphere of foreign policy. Redmond and his party made Home Rule Ireland an active and willing component of the British Empire by committing it to the war on Germany. Connolly, who commanded a small army formed during the 1913 Strike, and Roger Casement, who had an international reputation earned in the British diplomatic service, aligned themselves with Germany and declared for Irish independence.

The Volunteer movement as a whole remained united under Redmond's leadership throughout August and most of September. It had no foreign policy. It only split on September 25th, after Redmond's Woodenbridge speech. A very small minority (about 10,000 out of 200,000) then split off from Redmond. But they did not change sides in the war. They only objected to Redmond's new policy of stating the obvious fact that the coasts of Ireland were in no danger and urging the Volunteers to do their duty on the Continent.

Long before the Volunteer split, Connolly and Casement had aligned themselves with Germany and had determined to go to war against Britain. Their clarity of purpose was a major influence shaping events during the year and three quarters between the British declaration of war on Germany and the Irish declaration of war on Britain. Casement did not succeed in raising an Irish Brigade among the Irish prisoners-of-war in Germany, and Connolly's army never got very big, but their decisiveness at the start set the parameters for subsequent development. It was a powerful moral factor tending to counter-act the vacillations of the leaders of the dissident Volunteers, who acted at best on the *England's difficulty* principle. (To the best of my knowledge, nothing successful has ever been done on the basis of that principle.)

But Connolly and Casement had a world-view—by which I do not mean a high-sounding but vacuous maxim stuck onto the *England's difficulty* principle, but a view which actually encompassed the world and made real distinctions within it. And it is my impression that it is chiefly because their minds were well attuned to developments in the world at large—better attuned than the minds of the English ruling class—that the Easter Rising happened. I feel that, if all had been confined to the *England's difficulty* principle, England would have encountered little difficulty in Ireland, where nothing but grand fantasies would have occurred while the World War ran its course.

Connolly and Casement were both accustomed to exercise their own judgment on large matters, and to make decisions in the real world outside the walls of the Houses of Parliament on the basis of widely applicable principles. They were not narrow nationalists. Redmond, by contrast, *was* a narrow nationalist—one who had been flattered out of his mind by the Liberal Imperialists and taken in tow by them, and whose little horizons had been expanded by Imperial benevolence. And it does not seem to me that he or his colleagues ever gave a moment's real thought to the great war launched by Britain. They were mere tactical manipulators within the strategic ambit of British Parliamentary affairs, and the apparent success which they had achieved through the Parliamentary game rivetted them to British policy when Parliament authorised war on Germany—and made them agents of the Government in securing Parliamentary authorisation for that war.

Great events begin in the mind. The Great War began as a thought in the minds of Asquith, Haldane and Grey. If they had thought differently, it would not have happened. The counter-development which produced the Easter Rising also began in August 1914, in the minds of Connolly and Casement.

Clausewitz said in his famous maxim that war is the continuation of politics by other means. I found that maxim unsatisfactory and in **Derry And The Boyne** I reversed it. War, being the region of catastrophe, is more likely to be an end and a beginning than a continuation. Politics is the continuation of war by other means, in that it functions in the situation produced by war with a view to consolidating and developing it.

Clausewitz derived his maxim from the experience of the Napoleonic wars. Despite the length of those wars, the British ruling class sustained its original purpose throughout and in 1815 made a settlement more or less in accordance with its declared purpose at the start. One can see why Clausewitz formulated his maxim—and why, half a century later, Gladstone declared that "England has her constancy no less than Rome".

Bismarck, too, conducted his small wars with remarkable restraint and constancy of purpose, so that they appear to be phases of policy.

But Clausewitz's maxim ceases to apply on August 4th, 1914. A war of destruction against a major state, waged in the spirit of a war of religion, a war of good against evil, and with the possibility of a negotiated peace ruled out from the start—such a war throws everything into the melting pot. And its end is not in its beginning.

Redmond, not knowing what he did, gambled everything on the outcome of that reckless war. It seemed a safe bet because he was attaching himself to the big battalions. If the war had been won by Christmas, the Empire would have been consolidated and Ireland would very likely have been West Britain.

In Parliament, on September 15th, Redmond ridiculed "the men who are publishing little wretched rags once a week or once a month—which none of us ever see... If you take up these wretched rags you will find the praises of the Emperor of Germany in the same sentence as are denunciations of my colleagues and myself" (Hansard, cols 908/0). But, because the big battalions failed to deliver the goods on time, the wretched rags came into their own.

*

Casement and Childers ran guns to the Volunteers in late July 1914. In early August, Childers went off to participate in the war on Germany for which he had long been preparing the state. And Casement published **The Causes Of The War And The Foundation Of The Peace**. It was published in America in the autumn of 1914 and in Germany (as **The Crime Against Europe**) in 1915. It consisted chiefly of articles written during the three years before the war, some of which had been published under pseudonyms. The first, *The Keeper Of The Seas*, written in August 1911, summed up the probabilities of the situation as follows:

"The English mind, the English consciousness are such, that to oppose German influence in the world is to this people a necessity. They oppose by instinct, against argument, in the face of reason...

"Their reasoning, if reason exists in what is after all a matter of primal instinct, might find expression somewhat as follows: 'German influence cannot but be hostile to British interests. The two peoples are too much alike. The qualities that have made England great they possess in a still greater degree. Given a fair field and no favour they are bound to beat us. They will beat us out of every market in the world... Better to fight while we are still the stronger...'

"Some such obscure argument as this controls the Englishman's reasoning when he faces the growing magnitude of the Teutonic people...

"English Liberalism might desire a different sort of reckoning with Germany, but English Liberalism is itself a product of the English temperament, and however it may sigh, by individuals, for a better understanding between the two peoples, in the mass, it is a part of the national purpose and a phase of the national mind and is driven relentlessly to the rivets and the hammering, the 'Dreadnoughts' in being and that mightier Dreadnought yet to be, the Anglo-Saxon Alliance which Germany must fight if she is to get out."

Casement the most famous of British diplomats because of his Congo and Putamoyo reports, was well-acquainted with English ruling circles, and he observed them well. By his own account he made no secret of these views when he was amongst them. Nevertheless, they were genuinely shocked when in August 1914 he acted in accordance with those views. And perhaps those who were most shocked were those who, until the declaration of war, had more or less agreed with him, but who on August 5th found that for all their pretensions they really were only "a phase of the national mind".

The following extracts are from the article, **The Causes Of The War And The Foundation Of Peace**, written after the outbreak of war and dated, *"Philadelphia, 15th September, 1914"* (Casement was in America buying guns for the Volunteers when the war began)":

"To find the motive powerful enough to have plunged all Europe into war in the short space of a few hours, we must seek it, not in the pages of a 'white paper' covering a period of only fifteen days (July 20th to August 4th, 1914), but in the long anterior activities that led the great Powers of Europe into definite commitments to each other....

"Coming then to the five great combatants, we can quickly reduce them to four. Austria-Hungary and Germany in this war are indivisible. While each may have varying aims on many points and ambitions that, perhaps, widely diverge both have one common bond, self-preservation, that binds them much more closely together than mere formal 'allies'. In this war Austria fights of necessity as a Germanic Power, although the challenge to her has been on the ground of her Slav obligations and activities. Germany is compelled to support Austria by a law of necessity that a glance at the map of Europe explains....

"We thus arrive at the question, 'why should such strangely consorted allies as England, Russia and France be at war with the German people?'

"The answer is not to be found in the White Book, or in any statement publicly put forward by Great Britain, Russia or France.

"But the answer must be found, if we would find the causes of the war, and if we would hope to erect any lasting peace on the ruins of this world conflict.

"To accept, as an explanation of the war the statement that Germany has a highly trained army she has not used for nearly half a century and that her people are so obsessed with admiration for it that they longed to test it on their neighbours, is to accept as an explanation a stultifying contradiction. It is of course much easier to put the blame on the Kaiser. This line of thought is highly popular: it accords, too, with a fine vulgar instinct.

"The German people can be spared the odium of responsibility for a war they clearly did nothing to provoke, by representing them as the victims of an autocracy, cased in mail and beyond their control. We thus arrive at 'the real crime against Germany', which explains everything but the thing it set out to explain. It leaves unexplained the real crime against Europe.

"To explain the causes of war we must find the causes of the alliances of England, France and Russia against Europe.

"For the cause of the war is that alliance—that and nothing else. The defence of the *Entente Cordiale* is that it is an innocent pact of friendship, designed only to meet the threat of the Triple Alliance. But the answer to that is that whereas the Triple Alliance was formed thirty years ago, it has never declared war on anyone, while the *Triple Entente* before it is eight years old has involved Europe, America, Africa, and Asia in a world conflict....

"The *Entente Cordiale*, to begin with, is unnatural. There is nothing in common between the parties to it, save antagonism to someone else. It is wrongly named.... None of the parties to it like or admire each other, or have consistent aims, save one.

"That satisfied, they will surely fall out among themselves, and the greater the plunder derived from their victory the more certain their ensuing quarrel.

"Great Britain, in her dealings with most white people (not with all) is a democracy.

"Russia in her dealings with all, is an autocracy.

"Great Britain is democratic in her government of herself and in her dealings with the great white communities of Canada, Australia, New Zealand, and South Africa. She is not democratic in her dealings with subject races within the Empire...

"In both instances Britain is notably false to her professions of devotion to democratic principles. Her affinity with Russia is found then, not in the cases where her institutions are good, but in those where they are bad....

"The alliance with France, while more natural than that with Russia if we regard Great Britain as a democracy (by eliminating India, Egypt, Ireland) had the same guilty end in view, and rests less on affinity of aims than on affinity of antipathies.

"The *Entente Cordiale*, the more closely we inspect it, we find is based not on a cordial regard of the parties to it for each other, but on a cordial disregard all three participants share for the party it is aimed against.

"It will be said that Germany must have done something to justify the resentment that could bring about so strangely assorted a combination against herself. What has been the crime of Germany against the powers now assailing her? She has doubtless committed many crimes, as have all the great powers, but in what respect has she so grievously sinned against Europe that the Czar, the Emperor of India, the King of Great Britain and Ireland, the Mikado and the President of the French Republic—to say nothing of those minor potentates who like Voltaire's minor prophets seem *capable de tout*—should now be pledged, by irrevocable pact, to her destruction as a great power?

" 'German militarism', the reply that springs to the lips, is no more a threat to civilisation than French or Russian militarism. It was born, not of wars of aggression, but of wars of defence and unification. Since it was welded by blood and iron into the great human organism of the last forty years it has not been employed beyond the frontiers of Germany until last year.

"Can the same be said of Russian militarism or of French militarism or of British navalism?

"We are told the things differ in quality. The answer is what about the intent and the uses made. German militarism has kept the peace and has not emerged beyond its own frontier until threatened with universal attack. Russian militarism has waged wars abroad, far beyond the confines of Russian territory; French militarism, since it was overthrown at Sedan, has carried fire and sword across all Northern Africa, has penetrated the Atlantic to the Nile, has raided Tonquin, Siam, Madagascar, Morocco, while English navalism in the last forty years has bombarded the coast lines, battered the ports, and landed raiding parties throughout Asia and Africa, to say nothing of the well nigh continuous campaigns of annexation of the British army in India, Burma, South Africa, Egypt, Tibet, or Afghanistan, within the same period....

"...We are asked, however, to believe that French militarism is maintained by a 'democracy' and German militarism by an 'autocracy'. Without appealing to the captive Queen of Madagascar for an opinion on the authenticity of French democracy we may confine the question to the elected representatives of the two peoples.

"In both cases the war credits are voted by the legislative bodies responsible to French and German opinion. The elected representatives of Germany are as much the spokesman of the nation as those of France, and the German Reichstag has sanctioned every successful levy for the support of German armaments....

"For what does France, for what does Russia maintain a great army? Why does Germany call so many youthful Germans to the colours? On what grounds of moral sanction does Great Britain maintain a navy, whose cost far exceeds all the burdens of German militarism?...

"...No power can plunder or weaken Russia as long as she remains within her own borders. Of all the great powers in Europe she is the one that after England has the least need of a great army....

"The huge machine of the French army, its first line troops almost equal to Germany's, is not a thing of yesterday.

"It was not German aggression founded it—although Germany felt it once at Jena. Founded by kings of France, French militarism has flourished under republic, empire, constitutional monarchy, and empire again until to-day we find its greatest bloom full blown under the mild breath of the third republic. What is the purpose of this perfect machine? Self-defence? From what attack? Germany has had it in her power, again and again within the last thirty years to attack France at a disadvantage, if not even with impunity. Why has she refrained—whose hand retrained her? Not Russia's—not England's. During the Russo-Japanese war or during the Boer war, France could have been assailed with ease and her army broken to pieces. But German militarism refrained from striking that blow....

"We come now to the third party to the Entente... Until England appeared upon the scene neither Russia nor France, nor both combined, could summon up courage to strike the blow. Willing to wound they were both afraid to strike. It needed a third courage, a keener purpose and a greater immunity.

"German militarism was too formidable a factor in the life of 65,000,000 of the most capable people in Europe to be lightly assailed even by France and Russia combined....

"From the day that Great Britain and her mighty fleet joined the separated allies with their mighty armies, the bond between them and the circle around Germany grew taut....

"The sin of German militarism was at last out. It could take to the water as kindly as to the land. As long as the war machine guaranteed the inviolability of German territory it was no threat to European peace, but when it assumed the task of safe-guarding German rights at sea it became the enemy of civilization. These trading people not content with an army that kept French 'revanche' discreetly silent and Slav 'unity' a dream of the future presumed to have a sea-borne commerce that grew by leaps and bounds, and they dared to build a navy to defend and even to extend it. *Delenda est Carthago!* From that day the doom of 'German militarism' was sealed; and England, democratic England, lay down with the Czar in the same bed to which the French housewife had already transferred her republican counterpane....

"The mobilization by Russia was all that France needed 'to do that which might be required of her by her interests.' (Reply of the French Government to the German Ambassador at Paris, August 1st, 1914.)

"Had the neutrality of Belgium been respected as completely as the neutrality of Holland, England would have joined her 'friends' in the assault on Germany, as Sir Edward Grey was forced to admit when the German Ambassador in vain pressed him to state his own terms as the price of English neutrality....

"Such, in outline, are the causes and steps that led to the outbreak of war. The writer has seen those steps well and carefully laid, tested and tried beforehand....

"During the first six months of 1914, German export trade almost equalled that of Great Britain. Another year of peace, and it would certainly have exceeded it, and for the first time in the history of world trade Great Britain would have been put in the second place....

"Day by day as the war proceeds, although it is now only six weeks old, the pretences under which it was begun are being discarded. England fights not to defend the neutrality of Belgium, not to destroy German militarism, but to retain, if need be by involving the whole world in war, her supreme and undisputed ownership of the seas....

"British democracy loves freedom of he sea in precisely the same spirit as imperial Rome viewed the spectacle of Celtic freedom beyond the outposts of the Roman legions; as Agricola phrased it, something 'to wear down and take possession of so that freedom may be put out of sight'.... (The Crime Against Europe, p4-15.)

*

Casement knew at the outset where he stood on the war. He took it that the conflict would be between the existing states and had decided well before August 1914 that the survival of the German state against the efforts of the Triple Entente to destroy it was the most important thing in world politics.

Connolly came to a similar conclusion by late August 1914, when it became clear that the war was going to be fought between the existing states. But, in the first instance, he looked to class-based civil wars within each of the major states to prevent war between the states. He took it that the Socialist International was a real element in the political structure of Europe, and he looked to it to make some attempt to live up to its pre-war resolutions. In his article, **A Continental Revolution**, published in the Glasgow Independent Labour Party paper, **Forward** on August 16th, 1914, which seems to have been written before the British declaration of war, he said:

"The whole working class movement stands committed to war upon war—stands so committed at the very height of its strength and influence.

"And now, like a bolt from the blue, war is upon us, and war between the most important, because the most socialist, nations on earth. And we are helpless!

"What then becomes of all our resolutions, all our protests of fraternization, all our threats of general strikes, all our hopes of the future? Were they all sound and fury, signifying nothing? When the German artilleryman, a Socialist serving in the German Army of invasion, sends a shell into the ranks of the French Army, blowing off their heads, tearing out their bowels, and mangling the limbs of dozens of Socialist comrades in that force, will the fact that he, before leaving for the front, 'demonstrated' against the war be of any value to the widows and orphans made by the shell he sent upon its mission of murder?...

"But why go on? Is it not as clear as the fact of life itself that no insurrection of the working class, no general strike, no general uprising of the forces of Labour in Europe could possibly carry with it or entail a greater slaughter of Socialists than will their participation as soldiers in the campaigns of the Armies of their respective countries?... If these men must die, would it not be better to die in their own country fighting for freedom for their class, and for the abolition of war, than to go forth to strange countries and die slaughtering and being slaughtered by their brothers that tyrants and profiteers might live?

"Civilization is being destroyed before our eyes; the results of generations of propaganda and patient heroic plodding and self-sacrifice are being blown into annihilation from a hundred cannon mouths...

"I make no war upon patriotism; never have done. But against the patriotism of capitalism—the patriotism which makes the interests of the capitalist class the supreme test of duty and right—I place the patriotism of the working class, the patriotism which judges every public act by its effect upon the fortunes of those who toil...

"To me, therefore, the Socialist of another country is a fellow-patriot, as the capitalist of my own country is a natural enemy. I regard each nation as the possessor of a definite contribution to the common stock of civilisation, and I regard the capitalist class of each nation as being the logical and natural enemy of the national culture which constitutes that definite contribution...

"Reasoning from such premises, therefore, this war appears to me to be the most fearful crime of the centuries. In it the working class are to be sacrificed that a small clique of rulers and armament makers may sate their lust for power and their greed for wealth. Nations are to be obliterated, progress stopped, and international hatreds erected into the deities to be worshipped."

Connolly's initial attitude to the war was similar to Lenin's, even though his conceptual framework was very different. But, whereas Lenin maintained that, from a socialist viewpoint, there was nothing to choose between the states at war, Connolly had aligned himself with Germany by the end of that August, and he never wavered from that alignment. He did not take it to be a matter of indifference to the socialist cause which side won the war.

Because of the mode in which England went to war, there was in actuality a straight choice: England or Germany. Germany never had the destruction of England, or even of the British Empire, as its aim. But from the moment the war began, the minimal English war aim was the destruction of Germany. This was not an official war aim. There was no official war aim beyond the grand platitudes uttered around August 5th. The Cabinet does not seem to have discussed war aims at all until 1916, and then did so in a ragged and desultory manner. But the functional British war aim was set by the propaganda by which the ruling circle and its supporting intelligentsia excited the democracy for the war effort. Nothing less than the destruction of the German state and the humiliation of the German people would have satisfied the feelings generated in the democracy by the war propaganda, especially as the casualties mounted to unprecedented levels.

Seen in that context, the question was whether the cause of socialist development would be better served by the survival of Britain or the survival of Germany? Connolly gave his answer in **The War Upon The German Nation**, published in **The Irish Worker** of August 29, 1914:

"...I wish to try and trace the real origin of this war upon the German nation, for despite all the truculent shouts of a venal Press and conscienceless politicians, this war is not a war upon German militarism, but upon the industrial activity of the German nation.

"If the reader were even slightly acquainted with the history of industry in Europe he would know that as a result of the discovery of steam as a motive power, and the consequent development of machine industry depending upon coal, Great Britain towards the close of the eighteenth century began to dominate the commercial life of the world. Her large coal supply helped her to this at a time when the coal supply of other countries had not yet been discovered or exploited. Added to this was the fact that the ruling class of England by a judicious mixing in European struggles, by a dexterous system of alliances, and a thoroughly unscrupulous use of her sea power, was able to keep the Continent continually embroiled in war whilst her own shores were safe. Whilst the cities and towns of other countries were constantly the prey of rival armies, their social life crushed under the cannon wheels of contending forces, and their brightest young men compelled to give to warfare the intellect that might have enriched their countries by industrial achievements, England was able peacefully to build up her industries, to spread her wings of commerce, and to become the purveyor-general of manufactured goods to the civilized and uncivilized nations of the world. In her own pet phrase she was 'the workshop of the world,' and other nations were but as so many agricultural consumers of the products of England's factories and workshops.

"Obviously such a state of matters was grossly artificial and unnatural. It could not be supposed by reasonable men that the civilized nations would be content to remain for ever in such a condition of tutelage or dependence. Rather was it certain that self-respecting nations would begin to realize that the industrial overlordship by England of Europe meant the continued dependence of Europe upon England—a most humiliating condition of affairs.

"So other nations began quietly to challenge the unquestioned supremacy of England in the markets. They began first to produce for themselves what they had hitherto relied upon England to produce for them, and passed on from that to enter into competition with English goods in the markets of the world. Foremost and most successful European nation in this endeavour to escape from the thraldom of dependence upon England's manufactures stands the German nation. To this contest in the industrial world it brought all the resources of science and systematized effort. Early learning that an uneducated people is necessarily an inferior people, the German nation attacked the work of educating its children with such success that it is now universally admitted that the Germans are the best educated people in Europe. Basing its industrial effort upon an educated working class, it accomplished in the workshop results that this half-educated working class of England could only wonder at. That English working class, trained to a slavish subservience to rule-of-thumb methods, and under managers welded to traditional processes, saw themselves outclassed by a new rival in whose service were enrolled the most learned scientists co-operating with the most educated workers in mastering each new problem as it arose, and unhampered by old traditions, old processes, or old equipment. In this fruitful marriage of science and industry the Germans were pioneers, and if it seemed that in starting both they became unduly handicapped it was soon realized that if they had much to learn they had at least nothing to unlearn, whereas the British remained hampered at every step by the accumulated and obsolete survivals of past industrial competitions.

"Despite the long hold that England had upon industry, despite their pre-emption of he market, despite the influence of their far-flung empire, German competition became more and more a menace to England's industrial supremacy; more and more German goods took the place of English. Some few years ago the cry of "Protection" was raised in England in the hopes that English trade would be thus saved by a heavy customs duty against import commodities. But it was soon realized that as England was chiefly an exporting country a tax upon imported goods would not save her industrial supremacy. From the moment that realization entered into the minds of the British capitalist we may date the inception of this war.

"It was determined that since Germany could not be beaten in fair competition industrially, she must be beaten unfairly by organizing a military and naval conspiracy against her. British methods and British capitalism might be inferior to German methods and German capitalism; German scientists aided by German workers might be superior to British workers and tardy British science; but the British fleet was still superior to the German in point of numbers and weight of artillery. Hence it was felt that if the German nation could be ringed round with armed foes upon its every frontier until the British fleet could strike at its ocean-going commerce, then German competition would be crushed and the supremacy of England in commerce ensured for another generation. The conception meant calling up the forces of barbaric power to crush and hinder the development of the peaceful powers of industry. It was a conception worthy of fiends, but what do you expect? You surely do not expect the roses of honour and civilization to grow on the thorn tree of capitalist competition—and that tree planted in the soil of a British ruling class.

"But what about the independence of Belgium? Aye, what about it?

"Remember that the war found England thoroughly prepared, Germany totally unprepared. That the British fleet was already mobilized on a scale never attempted in times of peace, and the German fleet was scattered in isolated units all over the seven seas. That all the leading British commanders were at home ready for the emergency, and many German and Austrian officers, such as Slatin Pasha, have not beeh able to get home yet. Remember all this and realize how it reveals that the whole plan was ready prepared; and hence that the cry of 'Belgium' was a mere subterfuge to hide the determination to crush in blood the peaceful industrial development of the German nation. Already the British Press is chuckling with joy over the capture of 'German trade. All capitalist journals in England boast that the Hamburg-American Line will lose all its steamers, valued at twenty millions sterling. You know what that means! It means that a peaceful trade, built up by peaceful methods, is to be struck out of the hands of its owners by the sword of an armed pirate. You remember the words of John Mitchel descriptive of the British Empire as 'a pirate empire, robbing and plundering upon the high seas.'

"Understand the game that is afoot, the game that Christian England is playing, and when next you hear apologists for capitalism tell of the wickedness of Socialists in proposing to 'confiscate' property, remember the plans of

British and Irish capitalists to steal German trade—the fruits of German industry and German science.

"Yes, friends, Governments in capitalist society are but committees of the rich to manage the affairs of the capitalist class. The British capitalist class has planned this colossal crime in order to ensure its uninterrupted domination of the commerce of the world. To achieve that end it is prepared to bathe a continent in blood, to kill off the flower of the manhood of the three most civilized great nations of Europe, to place the iron heel of the Russian tyrant upon the throat of all liberty-loving races and peoples from the Baltic to the Black Sea, and to invite the blessing of God upon the spectacle of the savage Cossack ravishing the daughters of a race at the head of Christian civilization.

"Yes, this war is the war of a pirate upon the German nation.

"And up from the blood-soaked graves of the Belgian frontiers the spirits of murdered Irish soldiers of England call to Heaven for vengeance upon the parliamentarian tricksters who seduced them into the armies of the oppressor of their country."

Having concluded that a German victory in the war would be more conducive to socialist development than a British victory, Connolly gave extensive coverage in the final run of The Workers' Republic (1915-16) to the Right wing of German Social Democracy, which supported the German war effort. After August 1914 he treats the Left-wing of German Social Democracy as being of no account. I reprinted much of this material in a series of articles published in 1982, which were issued as a pamphlet in 1984 under the title, **Connolly Cut-outs**.

Two German philosophers appear in the Workers' Republic: Nietzsche and Rudolf Eucken. Some paragraphs from **Zarathustra** appear in an article on January 15th, 1916, with the comment that Nietzsche's writings "surpassed in originality and daring those of any other thinker in the nineteenth century". Rudolf Eucken, the most famous German philosopher of the time, is the subject of the article, **A German Philosopher On The War** on November 6th, 1915. Eucken, like Nietzsche, was a philosopher of the will.

A very long article with a German orientation, **War And Democracy**, by Meyrick Cramb, was serialised in The Workers' Republic on January 1st, 15th, 22nd and 29th, and February 5th, 1916. I have been unable to discover anything about Meyrick Cramb.

The Workers' Republic on February 19th carried, under the title, **The German State**, a long extract from a book by an American author, **Socialised Germany**, by Frederic C. Howe, describing how socialist forms of industry had been developing in the German mixed economy.

Connolly's most enduring Continental affinity was with Joseph Pilsudski's Polish Socialist Party. This affinity is strongly in evidence in both runs of The Workers' Republic (1898 and 1915-16). It was pointed out to me by Jack Lane, and I put all the material into current print in **Connolly: The Polish Aspect** (1985).

In the 1890s Pilsudski, like Connolly blended socialism with nationalism. He established the core of a Polish Legion before 1914 and in August 1914 he invaded the Tsarist Empire from Austrian Poland. After many adventures, military and political, the Polish state took its place in the post-war scheme of things, guaranteed by Pilsudski's army. And then in 1920, when Lenin tried to break out of his self-imposed isolation with a war of conquest through Poland towards Germany, his Red Army was broken outside Warsaw by Pilsudski.

Connolly was entirely in earnest in his view that the development of socialist civilisation depended on a German victory in the Great War. And the European socialist whom he most resembled was Pilsudski. Those two things are abundantly clear in his publications from August 1914 to Easter 1916. They were subsequently obscured by the political propagandists of other causes—in the first instance by Robert Lynd, the British war propagandist, and later by Leninist propagandists.

Labour In Irish History was first published by Maunsel in 1910. It was reissued by Maunsel in 1917, along with The Reconquest of Ireland, under the title, Labour In Ireland, with a biographical Introduction by Robert Lynd. The process of mystification, which still goes on today, was begun by Lynd in that Introduction (which is dated *October 1916*):

> "There are two questions that bewilder many people as they consider the last act of Connolly's career. They ask wonderingly how it came about that so good a European as Connolly could remain apparently indifferent to the German menace to European liberty. The second thing that puzzles them is that a man not merely of high character, but of strong intelligence, of experience in affairs, of, on the whole, orderly thought and speech—in fact, a man with his head as sound as his heart—should have consented to throw himself into a design so obviously incapable of success as the Easter rising. As to the former question, the answer is probably simple enough. Connolly could not interest himself very deeply in a war which he interpreted, I imagine, as a struggle between one group of capitalist governments and another."

Maunsel was a publishing company set up by a group of Anglo-Irish philanthropists, sympathetic to Irish Home Rule, but firmly aligned with Britain in world affairs. Stephen Gwynn, one of its founders, wrote Home Rule pamphlets before the war and war propaganda during the war.

Lynd, as a student in Belfast, had known Connolly briefly in 1898 but does not seem to have been greatly impressed by him. His brief in the 1916 Introduction was damage limitation—limitation of the damage done to the British war effort by Connolly's participation in the Rising. The means he chose was to disparage Connolly with backhanded praise. He represented Connolly as a very earnest but also very simple-minded socialist who sympathised intensely with the misery of the poor and who hit out blindly at the local oppressors of the poor when the opportunity for doing so presented itself. International affairs lay beyond the reach of his imagination:

> "we may be sure that the German War appeared to him as a mere riot among the governments of Europe without significance for the labouring poor. It is clear at any rate that he did not agree with those of us who took the view that a victory for Germany which would give her the mastery of the seas would end in a German conquest and colonisation of Ireland, which would be still more efficiently destructive than the English conquest. He was so intensely preoccupied with the necessity of getting rid of the twofold burden of foreign rule and capitalism... that a hypothetical German conquest may have seemed to him merely a phantom. In any case the whole energy of his mind had always been absorbed in the struggle between governments and peoples, not in the struggle between governments and governments, or even in the struggle between peoples and peoples. Probably he would have denied that a war between two real democracies is possible. And indeed if European society had been based on the Socialistic principles advocated by Connolly, even a blind man must see that the present war would never have taken place."

Had Lynd taken so little interest in what Connolly had been publishing since the start of the war that he believed what he said in this Introduction? Or was he doing an honest job of lying in the service of the Empire whose world dominance he saw as being necessary to civilisation? There may somewhere be correspondence between Lynd and Maunsel that would shed some light on this question. But it has suited all historians and biographers up to the present not to see that there is a question, and so it has never been asked.

(Lynd became an immensely popular writer in England after the war. For thirty years he published an annual book of essays in which he dealt with whatever caught his fancy, but I don't think he ever again mentioned Connolly. This would suggest that his 1916 effort was a cold-blooded piece of propaganda work.)

Lynd rounds off his Introduction by giving the last word on Connolly to T.M. Kettle:

"The question of Connolly's mood and purpose in the insurrection is one to which one returns in perplexity again and again. The most convincing answer I got was from T.M. Kettle when I saw him in Dublin last July. 'No', he said, 'I don't think Connolly expected to win... It seems to me that if you want to explain Connolly you can only do so on the lines of that poem of Francis Adams's, 'Anarchists'...

"'Connolly', he went on, 'felt the intolerable outrage of the triumph of—

"'The husk-hearted Gentleman
And the mud-hearted Bourgeois'

"Then Kettle slowly repeated with that deliberate passionate eloquence, which made his melancholy seem at times not a weakness but a power, the last verse of the poem—

"'—a sombre hateful desire
Burns up slow in my breast
To wreck the great guilty Temple
And give us rest!'

"That seems to me to be the true interpretation of the last passion of James Connolly."

All's fair in love and war they say. And certainly all who were drawn into British war propaganda in the Great War lost all sense of fair play.

Within the nationalist movement, Kettle was a leading Hibernian. Connolly detested Hibernianism, which he saw as the Catholic counter-part of Orangeism. Internationally, Kettle led the British imperialist mob which were baying for the destruction of Germany. Giving Kettle the last word on Connolly was therefore an act of gross indecency.

The act of indecency was continued by the Communist Party, which since 1967 has been reprinting Labour In Irish History along with Lynd's Introduction. Connolly, whose long-term European alignment was with Pilsudski and who in the critical period of 1914-16 also aligned himself with the right-wing of German social democracy, was selected by Leninism for reconstruction on Leninist lines. Given the fundamental disparity of outlook and policy between Connolly and Lenin, this could only be done through much mystification and bamboozlement. Desmond Greaves, whose weighty Leninist biography shaped the writings of all subsequent biographers, built on the confusion developed in the first instance by Lynd.

Within the Leninist movement there has been a discernible West British strain which feels that, if Connolly had to deviate from Leninism in his war policy, he really ought to have deviated on the other side. John de Courcy Ireland is an example. In 1991 he addressed a Robert Lynd Summer School in Belfast, expressing his great admiration for Lynd and uttering not a word in criticism of his war propaganda. But on a number of occasions he has sniped at Connolly's alignment with Germany:

"I have to confess that if you read what Connolly was writing in 1916 it is a bit alarming. It really is a bit alarming. Connolly was writing as though he had come that much under the influence of Pearse, he was able to talk about Germany, seven years before the rise of the Nazi party, as though it was some kind of Utopia, and his praise of the German people and his contemptuous dismissal of Servians and other people who were fighting for their independence at the time and who had a record as good as ours, is frightening to read" (**Revolutionary Movements Of The Past**, Repsol Pamphlet, 1971, p26).

The independent Irish state originated in a difference of opinion amongst nationalists about the character of the Great War. The 1916 Proclamation sanctions the alignment taken up by Casement and Connolly, with its reference to "gallant allies in Europe". And I should have thought that the fact that Connolly was of the opinion that the best prospect for socialism lay in a German victory would have been sufficient reason for later generations of socialists at least to try to understand why he held that opinion. Unfortunately, the socialist movement in nationalist Ireland has at best been only a West British hangover. It has never dared to work through the implications of the separation from Britain. And it has treated Connolly as an icon, ignoring the substance of his views, or, where it has taken some notice of his views, it has travestied them, as De Courcy Ireland has done.

Connolly made out a good case for regarding Germany as the state in which democratic socialism was most developed. Thirty years ago it might have seemed that, however good that case was in its time, conditions had changed so much that it no longer applied. But today, when Leninist socialism has collapsed due to sheer human inadequacy, and when Britain has chosen to have thirteen years of actively anti-socialist government, those social qualities of Germany which Connolly admired can be seen to have been durable. Thatcherism in Britain, busily dismantling socialism at home, is desperately resisting what it sees as as socialism being reimposed on it by a European political structure of which Germany is the chief component. And Irish socialists have for the most part been aligned with Thatcherite Britain against Europe. Perhaps now that this point of absurdity has been reached, there will be a willingness to take Connolly's views on Europe more seriously than they have ever been taken heretofore.

*

The purpose of this book is to locate the Irish independence movement in its actual historical context of the Great War. The Home Rule movement, acting as the virtual government of Ireland, declared war on Germany in association with Liberal Imperialist Britain. The independence movement began in an act of dissent against the war on Germany and culminated in an act of war against Britain in alliance with Germany. But the Irish state has thus far not had the moral courage to establish a place for itself in the world which accords with its origins.

I have glanced at a couple of histories by fashionable historians published recently. Roy Foster says that "the scenario for 1916 was created almost entirely by another extraneous event: the First World War" (**Modern Ireland**, Penguin edn, p461). The Home Rule and Ulster Unionist leaders were both thoroughly implicated in the decision to make war on Germany and they competed with each other in recruiting cannon fodder for the war. Irish casualties in that war far exceeded the combined total of casualties in the Easter Rising, the War of Independence and the Civil War. Yet Foster can see the Great War as an "extraneous event" in the life of Ireland. It is a curious conception.

Joseph Lee also in effect treats the war as an extraneous event, as a kind of upheaval of nature. He says nothing about the character of the war itself, but only discusses whether Redmond took the best tactical advantage of it: "Whatever Redmond's motives, and however far he may have been swayed by a genuine if imaginative conviction that Britain was fighting 'in defence of right, of freedom and of religion' there were strong tactical arguments in favour of his attitude, even from a separatist viewpoint. Any other policy would have played straight into the hands of Ulster Unionists" (**Ireland 1912-1988**, 1989, p21).

Foster's view is bizarre, but Lee's is appalling. Redmond's only excuse for funnelling the Irish nation into the British army to be wasted in the mad war to destroy Germany was that he believed the Liberal Imperialist assertion that it was a war to save civilisation. If he had done it merely as a tactic to gain a debating point against the Ulster Unionists, he should be seen as a kind of political psychopath. (But Professor Lee is himself pretty unbalanced on the subject of Ulster Unionists. His book begins with a racist diatribe against them.)

*

There has been much chatter in recent years about blood sacrifice and irrationalism in connection with 1916. The cultural forces which have been uppermost in Irish life during recent decades are psychologically adapted to being at ease with whatever Britain takes responsibility for, however horrendous it is, and to being uneasy about whatever is not done on Britain's moral credit.

Once the Allies failed to outflank the Germans of the Battle of the Marne in Autumn 1914, four years of mass killing followed, which would have been considered irrational in the extreme if Britain had not invested its immense moral credit in the world to surround it with an aura of rationality. The German offensive had miscarried. The German front was in danger of collapse. But with unprecedented ingenuity and determination the German Army extemporised strong defensive positions right up to the sea. Thereafter, Germany was strategically on the defensive and the possibility of negotiated settlement lay entirely with the Allies. The British Cabinet never for a moment contemplated a negotiated settlement. For four years the Anglo-French Armies pushed against the German line in episodes which are called battles, but which have no resemblance to any battles fought before or since. Masses of infantry were flung against the German position in battles which lacked any real territorial objective, and whose only purpose was to reduce the German population. They were battles in which nothing counted but the killing. And the Allies could incur heavier losses than the Germans and still consider that they were winning, so long as they had a statistically better rate of attrition proportionate to population than the Germans. (The Germans, having a smaller population to draw on, might lose fewer men in these encounters and yet lose a bigger part of the population.)

After a couple of years, the French lost the taste for this kind of war, and would probably have given up the war and negotiated a settlement. Unfortunately, they had their morale stiffened by the British, who relished it.

A couple of months after the Easter Rising the 'Battle of the Somme' was launched. On the first day, the British Army alone suffered 20,000 dead, and it continued for months. Company after company climbed out of their trenches and marched slowly into machine-gun fire during a long summer day. *That* was blood sacrifice. As between those who went over the top at the Somme, and those who came out in Easter 1916, there can be no real doubt which were the more careful of their lives.

But, since we are a very literary people, perhaps it's the poetry of blood sacrifice that our neo-Redmondites have in mind. Well, it was Rupert Brooke who started it, thanking God for matching him with the hour for killing Germans. And there is a poem by Asquith's son, Herbert, who served throughout the war in France and relished it. It is called **The Volunteer** and was quite famous in its time:

"Here lies a clerk who half his life had spent
Toiling at ledgers in a city grey,
Thinking that so his days would drift away
With no lance broken in life's tournament:
Yet ever 'twixt the books and his bright eyes
The gleaming eagles of the legions came,

And horsemen charging under phantom skies,
Went thundering past within the oriflamme.

"And now those waiting dreams are satisfied;
From twilight into spacious dawn he went;
His lance is broken; but he lies content
With that high hour, in which he lived and died.
And falling thus he wants no recompense,
Who found his battle in the last resort;
Nor heeds he any hearse to bear him hence,
Who goes to join the men of Agincourt."

How's that for the barbaric vision of life surviving under the aesthetic veneer of
The Souls?

This was published in **The Volunteer And Other Poems**, 1915. And, in
another poem in that collection, *The Western Line, Flanders, 1915*, we read:

"Above the clouds what lights are gleaming?
    God's batteries are those,
Or souls of soldiers homeward streaming
    To banquet with their foes?
The floods of battle ebb and flow.
The soldiers to Valhalla go!
...
The fighting men go charging past,
    With battle in their eyes,
The fighting men go reeling past,
    Like gods in poor disguise."

I don't know that Pearse actually sent anybody to Valhalla. But Asquith
glorified war amidst the carnage of it.
                    *

Another groundless argument much heard in recent years concerns mandates.
It is said that the insurrectionaries acted in defiance of the democratic mandate
given to the Home Rule Party by the electorate. I have never seen the fact
mentioned that the Parliamentary mandate given to the Home Rule Party in 1910
ran out in 1915. The Parliament Act of 1911, which enabled the Lords' veto on
the Home Rule Bill to be overcome, also reduced the life of Parliament from seven
years to five. The Parliamentary mandate ran out in December 1915. From then
until the end of 1918 there was only the conflict of arbitrary forces.

Since England was immersed in an absorbing war—a moral crusade in defence
of civilisation no less—it would perhaps be a far-fetched debating point to say that
it was subject to arbitrary government from 1915 to 1918. Other peoples, finding
themselves under the necessity of fighting wars, have tried to do so as efficiently
as possible. But England has not fought any war out of necessity since the Spanish
Armada (leaving aside its own Civil War of the 1640s), and yet it has fought more
wars than any other state during that time. I can only conclude from this that war
is a pleasure which England imposes on itself as a duty. And I don't think that an
electoral distraction from the war would have been popular in England in 1915.

There is a complex empirical relationship between Parliament and society in
England. Wolfe Tone recognised two hundred years ago that England had the
substance of representative government, even under the undemocratic franchise
of the time. And, though formal democracy was introduced in the course of the

19th century, the older substantive relationship between Parliament and society has persisted. Parliamentary majorities in other regions of the State count for less than extra-Parliamentary pressures in England. A recent example is the Poll Tax. Scotland had to have it, although it did not vote for it, because it was willed in accordance with the formal democracy of the state. England voted for it, but then decided that it disliked it, so it was withdrawn under extra-Parliamentary pressure. Thus England may bind other regions of the state by its formal mandate. But, when it feels that it has made a mistake in its electoral behaviour, it is not bound by its own mandate—it resorts to the older habits of substantive representation to overrule its votes.

In 1915, the formal electoral mandate of Parliament ran out. Parliament extended its life by virtue of its empirical relationship with English society. But it did not have that kind of relationship with Ireland. Therefore I can see no reasonable grounds for the assumption that the Home Rule Party had an electoral mandate after December 1915.

I think the Insurrection of 1916 should be seen as an arbitrary rebellion against an arbitrary Government. The Government had set aside the democratic process for the purpose of waging a great war. So let us forget about mandates. There were no mandates. There was only the war.

Note. I have been obliged by hospitalisation to curtail this Epilogue, but I hope to resume this theme in a further book which will see the war through to its end, both in its Irish and European dimensions, and carry through to post-war British behaviour in the League of Nations, in its oldest colony, Ireland, and in its newest colony, Iraq. I have been able to complete this book for printing, insofar as it has been completed, only because of the handsome treatment I received from the staff of Ward 7 South, Belfast City Hospital.

Belfast City Hospital,
August 1992.

Appendixes

1. Margot Asquith

[After the body of the book was typeset, I managed to find a copy of Margot Asquith's **Autobiography**, first published in 1922. The extracts given below are from Volume 2, Chapter VII:]

...on Wednesday the 29th [1914] I went to rest before dinner earlier than usual; but I could not sleep... At 7.30 pm the door opened and Henry came into my bedroom. I saw at once by the gravity of his face that something had happened...

"I have sent the precautionary telegram to every part of the Empire", he said, "informing all the Government Offices... that they must prepare for war. We have been considering this for the last two years at the Committee of Defence..."

Deeply moved, and thrilled with excitement, I observed the emotion on his face and said "Has it come to this!" At which he nodded without speaking, and after kissing me left the room.

The next day I went to the Speaker's Gallery... Before going into the Gallery, Henry and I met for a moment alone, and I asked him if things were really so alarming. To which he replied: "Yes, I'm afraid they are: our fellows don't all agree with me about the situation, but times are too serious for any personal consideration and whether X—— or Z—— do or do not resign matters little to me, as long as Crewe and Grey are there: I don't intend to be caught napping."

I remembered vaguely the frigid acknowledgement of some of the Ulster aristocracy and a withdrawal of skirts as I took my seat in the closely packed Gallery and watched my husband with throbbing pulses as he rose to his feet.

...

When he sat down there was a look of bewilderment amounting to awe upon every member's face. I got up to go but the fashionable females crowded round me, pressing close and asking questions. "Good Heavens! Margot!" they said, "what can this mean? Don't you realise the Irish will be fighting each other this very night? How fearfully dangerous! What does it mean?"

The Orange aristocracy, who had been engaged in strenuous preparations for their civil war and had neither bowed nor spoken to me for months past, joined in the questioning. Looking at them without listening and answering as if in a dream, I said: "We are on the verge of a European War."

The next day, Friday the 31st, while I was breakfasting in bed, my husband came to see me... I looked anxiously at his face; but he said that he himself had given up all hope...

He arrived late at the House, having been kept by an interview with business men in the city. "They are the greatest ninnies I have ever had to tackle", he said. "I found them all in a state of funk, like old women chattering over tea cups in a Cathedral town"...

We were still worried over the Irish question, and after dinner I wrote a line to Mr. Redmond telling him that he had the opportunity of his life of setting an unforgettable example to the Carsonites if he would go to the House of Commons on the Monday and in a great speech offer all his soldiers to the Government; or, if he preferred it, write and offer them to the King. It appeared to me that it would be a dramatic thing to do at such a moment, and might strengthen the claim of Ireland upon the gratitude of the British people.

On Sunday morning, August the 2nd, he replied to me in the following letter:

"18 Wynnstay Gardens
Kensington

"Dear Mrs. Asquith—I received your letter late last night. I am very grateful to you for it. I hope to see the Prime Minister to-morrow before the House meets if only for a few moments and I hope I *may be able* to follow your advice. With sincere sympathy. I am very truly yours, J.E. Redmond. *Sunday 2 Aug. 1914.*"

...

Mr. Montague dined with us that night... "Till last night", he said, "I had hoped against hope that we might have been able to keep out of this war, but my hopes have vanished. All the men I've seen feel like me except X——, who is intriguing with that scoundrel Z—— . I asked the Attorney General yesterday what was going to be said upon specie in the House to-morrow, and he said: "Don't worry! none of us can say at this moment what resignations the Prime Minister may or may not have in his hands at to-morrow's Cabinet."

Feeling profoundly indignant I thought of saying: "All right! You can warn these men that nothing will affect my husband; he will form a Coalition with the other side and then they will be done for"; but, as there was no one whose judgement I particularly valued on the Opposition benches, I refrained.... We were interrupted by O—— coming into the room... I asked him if it was really true that X—— was intriguing with the Pacifists, to which O—— replied: "He has always loathed militarism, as you know, since the days of the Boer War, and has an inferior crowd around him, but until he knows how much backing he will have in the country, I doubt if he will commit himself...

"It is always interesting to speculate on the motives that move men, and after considerable experience I have come to the conclusion that self-love or self-consciousness of some kind lies at the root of most resignations. Unselfcentred people do not suffer from the same temptations: they are simple and disengaged, willing to help and ready to combine or stand aside...

We had men of every temperament and every persuasion in our Government: orators, windbags, funks and fighters, Jews, Celts and non-Conformists. I have never understood why anyone should be proud of having either Jewish or Celtic blood in their veins. I have had, and still have, devoted friends among the Jews, but have often been painfully reminded of the saying, "A Jew is round your neck, at your feet, but never by your side"; Celtic blood is usually accompanied by excited brains and reckless temperament... When not whining or wheedling, the Celt is usually in a state of bluff or funk, and can always wind himself up to the kind of rhetoric that no housemaid can resist...

The Liberal Party has always hated Force, and love of Peace is what their opponents most dislike in them.

It is not easy for any Prime Minister to commit his Party to a war on foreign soil with an unknown foe, but it was lucky for this country that the Liberals were in power in 1914, as men might have been suspicious of acquiescing in such a terrible decision at the dictation of a Jingo government...

[And on August 4th:] I left to go to bed, and, as I was pausing at the foot of the staircase, I saw Winston Churchill with a happy face striding towards the double doors of the Cabinet room."

2. Churchill

[Churchill wrote as follows in **The World Crisis:**]

The Cabinet on Friday afternoon sat long revolving the Irish problem. The Buckingham Palace Conference had broken down. The disagreements and antagonisms seemed as fierce and as hopeless as ever, yet the margin in dispute, upon which such fateful issues hung, was inconceivably petty. The discussion turned principally upon the boundaries of Fermanagh and Tyrone. To this pass had the Irish factions in their insensate warfare been able to drive their respective British champions. Upon the disposition of these clusters of humble parishes turned at that moment the political future of Great Britain. The North would not agree to this, and the South would not agree to that. Both the leaders wished to settle; both had dragged their followers forward to the utmost point they dared. Neither seemed able to give an inch. Meanwhile, the settlement of Ireland must carry with it an immediate and decisive abatement of party strife in Britain, and those schemes of unity and co-operation which had so intensely appealed to the leading men on both sides, ever since Mr. Lloyd George had mooted them in 1910, must necessarily have come forward into the light of day. Failure to settle on the other hand meant something very like civil war and the plunge into depths of which no one could make any measure. And so, turning this way and that in search of an exit from the deadlock, the Cabinet toiled around the muddy byways of Fermanagh and Tyrone. One had hoped that the events of April at the Curragh and in Belfast would have shocked British public opinion, and formed a unity sufficient to impose a settlement on the Irish factions. Apparently they had been insufficient. Apparently the conflict would be carried one stage further by both sides with incalculable consequences before there would be a recoil. Since the days of the Blues and the Greens in the Byzantine Empire, partisanship had never been carried to more absurd extremes. An all-sufficient shock was, however, at hand.

The discussion had reached its inconclusive end, and the Cabinet was about to separate, when the quiet grave tones of Sir Edward Grey's voice were heard reading a document which had just been brought to him from the Foreign Office. It was the Austrian note to Serbia. He had been reading or speaking for several minutes before I could disengage my mind from the tedious and bewildering debate which had just closed. We were all very tired, but gradually as the phrases and sentences followed one another, impressions of a wholly different character began to form in my mind. This note was clearly an ultimatum,; but it was an ultimatum such as had never been penned in modern times. As the reading proceeded it seemed absolutely impossible that any State in the world could accept it, or that any acceptance, however abject, would satisfy the aggressor. The parishes of Fermanagh and Tyrone faded into the mists and squalls of Ireland, and a strange light began immediately, but by perceptible gradations, to fall and grow upon the map of Europe. [Volume 1, Chapter IX, pp154/5 of 1938 Edition.]

[In a letter to Venetia Stanley, July 28, 1914, Asquith wrote as follows about Churchill's state of mind:]
...What you say à propos of the War cutting off one's head to get rid of a headache is very good. Winston on the other hand is all for this way of escape from Irish troubles, and when things looked rather better last night, he exclaimed moodily that it looked after all as if we were in for a 'bloody peace'!...

3. G.B. Shaw

In November 1914, G.B. Shaw published as a supplement to the **New Statesman** a long article entitled, **Common Sense About The War**. It caused a small sensation at the time because it was discordant with the high moral tone of the war propaganda. But it was an entirely safe sensation of the kind favoured by Shaw as a method of self-advertisement. He showed that he had not been taken in by the official account of why Britain declared war, and that he understood that, while Belgian neutrality was an advantageous excuse, Britain would have declared war on Germany, even if it had not touched Belgium. Of the ogre, Bernhardi, he said: "He shews in the clearest way that if Germany does not smash England, England will smash Germany by springing at her the moment she can catch her at a disadvantage. In a word he prophesies that we, his great masters in *Realpolitik*, will do precisely what our Junkers have just made us do. It is we who have carried out the Bernhardi program: it is Germany who has neglected it."

Then, having demonstrated that he had not been taken in by the war propaganda, he supported the British war effort on the ground that "Prussian Militarism" needed to be taken down a peg.

Then he made this practically meaningless qualification: "The war should be pushed vigorously, not with a view to a final crushing of the German army between the Anglo-French combination and the Russian millions, but to the establishment of a decisive military superiority by the Anglo-French combination alone. A victory unattainable without Russian aid would be a defeat for Western European Liberalism: Germany would be beaten not by us but by a Military autocracy worse than her own". And, "Neither England nor Germany must claim moral superiority in the negotiations."

By November 1914 these were already absurd suggestions. Britain was fighting a war without limited aims and therefore without any prospect of a negotiated end. Its only aim, determined by the propaganda by which British society was energised for the fight, was the destruction of the evil German state and the punishment of the German people with a view to rooting out the source of that evil.

The war was begun in military alliance with Tsarist Russia, and the proposal that the Western Allies should break that alliance in order that Western Liberalism should have an uncompromised victory was one that could not be acted on in the real world. But in the event the war *was* won by the Western Allies alone, due to the internal collapse of Tsarist Russia in 1917. If Tsarist Russia had survived to be present at Versailles, the post-war Treaty would certainly have been much better. The presence of a powerful Russian state among the victors would probably have caused Britain and France to act much more prudently towards Germany.

4. Frank Harris (Author of *My Life And Loves*)

[The following extracts are from Harris's England Or Germany, 1915:]

Some of the best heads in the world have written about this war, and yet no one stands out as having approached impartiality... The Germans all believe that they have been attacked... On the other hand, the Allies consider Germany the aggressor: Anatole France throws down his pen and enlists at nearly seventy to fight the 'barbarians'; Wells professes to regard the Germans as 'inferior' beings...; even Bernard Shaw appears to have regretted his attempt to see things as they really are and agrees that the Germans must be crushed. And now comes M. Faguet, eager to show that a really eminent critic may also be blinded by prejudice.

He begins by stating that the Germans are hated by all nations, and he infers therefrom that they are hateworthy... Mr. Faguet appears to have no notion of the fact that men are apt to hate their superiors just as they like their inferiors; in proportion as a man rises above the ordinary he is sure to be disliked... The Germans are hated because they have done great things in the last twenty years; they are not only strong in the military sense, but they have shown themselves as successful in business as in music and philosophy. their population and wealth have grown by leaps and bounds, and, strange to say, they have been wise enough at the same time to do away with poverty. Much less would have sufficed to earn them general dislike, even if their manners had been as urbane and distinguished as they are reputed to be rude and aggressive.

Partisans, especially English-speaking, are pretty sure to condemn this book of mine as if it were written in a spirit of bitter prejudice. There is probably an inclination in me to take the weaker side, the side of those who have the odds against them, for I have often noticed this inclination in other Celts;... In self-justification I say that those who would stand upright must lean against the prevalent wind in proportion to its strength.

...I had practically written this book before I came across the "Englische Fragmente" of Heine. I was astounded to find that the conclusions to which Heine came after visiting England three-quarters of a century ago were almost exactly the conclusions which had gradually forced themselves in on me and I had set down after living and working twenty-five years in the country. Now Heine was a Jew, and apt, as must Jews are, to honour success and material prosperity such as England possesses, unduly; yet Heine condemns the English laws and the modern English ideals as passionately as I do: Jew and Celt examining the subject form opposite viewpoints and arriving at the same result!

We both condemn the English oligarchy, English snobbishness and English hypocrisy; we are struck with horror by the incredible cruelty with which the English treat the poor, and unimaginable savagery of their laws, mainly directed against the weak. It was Heine who taught Matthew Arnold to see the "degradation of the English working class", "the ignorance and sordid narrow-mindedness of their middle-class", and the "barbarism" of their nobility. Heine left England, he tells us, to get away from "gentlemen" and live among ordinary knaves and fools...

Yet, though I agree with Heine in his condemnation of much in England, I differ from him in having some hope. The vices of the English governing class and the savagery of their laws only serve to set in relief the fact that such of their working-class enjoy decent conditions of life are among the finest specimens of humanity to be met with anywhere... [p4-6.]

Shortly before the war, Mr. H.G. Wells, in his book entitled **Social Forces In England And America**, wrote as follows:
"We in Great Britain are now intensely jealous of Germany... not only because the Germans outnumber us, and have a much larger and more diversified country than ours..., but because in the last hundred years, while we have fed on platitudes and vanity, they have had the energy and humility to develop a splendid system of national education, to toil at science and art and literature, to develop social organisation, to master and better our methods of business and industry, and to clamber above us in the scale of civilization. This has humiliated and irritated rather than chastened us..."
Since the commencement of the war, Mr. Wells has changed his tune. He now says:
"That trampling, drilling foolery in the heart of Europe that has arrested civilization for forty years, German imperialism and German militarism, has struck its inevitable blow." [Ibid, p10.]

The yearly bill of the German State for the care of its sick, injured and aged amounts to thirty four millions sterling; whereas in England under the Workmen's Compensation Act, while less than three million sterling is paid in compensation, four millions a year go in expenses. Germany spends on social services 50 per cent more than on her army and navy." [p15.]

Germany is a curious amalgam of a hierarchy framed and fitted for war grafted on democratic institutions and inspired in civil life by an intensely democratic spirit of equality and willingness to work—a sort of despotism with strong socialistic tendencies. [p168.]

5. Gilbert Murray

There is an old saying that truth is the first casualty in war. But that saying is only true up to a point. There is a kind of routine lying for the purpose of misleading the enemy command and keeping up morale and it rarely goes beyond that. Nations at war are usually careful not to subvert their own culture with the lies they tell for war purposes. The distinctive thing about British propaganda in the Great War is that it was militarily effective in a way that was culturally self-destructive. What Britain did to itself in making war on Germany rendered it unfit to exercise the world dominance which was its only rational object in that war.

It was through Gilbert Murray that I first got an inkling of what had happened to the imperial mind of Britain in 1914. A few years ago, I chanced upon a pamphlet he wrote for the *Oxford War Pamphlets* series in the autumn of 1914. I am very rarely surprised by human behaviour and am hardly ever shocked be it. But I was thoroughly shocked by Murray's pamphlet. Because of "the nightmare doctrines of Bismarck, Nietzsche and Bernardi", he wrote, "I find that I do desperately desire to hear of German dreadnoughts sunk in the North Sea. Mines are treacherous engines of death; but I would be glad to help in laying a mine for them. When I see one day that 20,000 Germans have been killed in such-and-such an engagement, and the next day that it was only 2,000, I am sorry." (**Thoughts On The War**, October, 1914. Oxford War Pamphlets No. 41.)

Murray was Professor of Greek at Oxford before the war, during the only period when English academic life produced intellectuals comparable to the Germans. I was never at Oxford and I know no Greek, but I came across Murray's translations of Euripides back in the fifties and some of them stayed in my head thereafter. In Slieve Luacra society, where I lived to the age of twenty-one, poetry had nothing to do with education. It was part of the general culture and therefore was easily memorised, and it stuck around in the head as a kind of bass accompaniment to whatever the intellect was doing. I found Murray's translation

107

of the choruses of The Bacchae particularly striking and can recall them thirty-five years later. A chorus on the Bacchic orgy begins:

"Will they ever come to me again,
The long, long dances,
On through the dark till the dim stars wane?
Will I feel the dew on my throat, and the stream
Of wind in my hair? Shall our white feet gleam
In the dim expanses."

And the Bacchic philosophy:

"Happy he on the weary sea
Who hath fled the tempest and won the haven,
Happy he who hath risen free
Above his striving: for strangely graven
Is the orb of life, that one and another
In gold and power shall outpass his brother;
And men in their millions float and flow
And seethe with a million hopes as leaven;
And they win their will, or they miss their will,
And their hopes are dead or are pined for still;
But whoe'er shall know,
As the long days go,
That to live is happy has found his heaven."

There's no accounting for poetry or music, and there's no explaining why I knew when I came across Murray expressing sadness when 20,000 dead Germans were reduced to 2,000 that I was in the presence of a profound and extensive cultural tragedy—a British tragedy which was also a tragedy for the world because of the place Britain had gained in it.

5. Colonel Repington

Lieut.-Col. C. à Court Repington, the military correspondent of The Times, was much more than a journalist. He held a position in the military-political establishment which no military correspondent has ever held since. For one thing he had a room at the War Office. The active part which he played in the Curragh Mutiny led to a formal distancing of his relationship with the Government, but in reality he remained very much an insider in the ruling circle of the establishment.

Haldane's reorganisation of the Army from 1906 onwards was accompanied by what I think it is fair to call a militarisation of society. While there was no conscription, and the Army continued to be composed of volunteers or mercenaries (depending on how you look at it), the development of the Territorial Army made militarism an influential component of ordinary life in England. And the state fostered the discussion of military affairs at a popular level in a way that I do not think had previously been done in England. The regular army then took on the character of a cadre force which, when the occasion arose, could quickly shape large quantities of enthusiastic recruits into fighting formations.

The generation of a militarist spirit in society had been so thorough that a war effort on an unprecedented scale was sustained for two years without conscription.

The propaganda preparation for the war took many forms. One of them was the lectures to Aldershot Military Society which were published in popular format in the *Aldershot Military Society Pamphlets* series. Repington delivered two of these lectures. In the first (**Peace Strategy**, January 30, 1907, chaired by General Sir John French) he explained the difference between Peace Strategy and War Strategy. War Strategy has to do with the conduct of forces in battle and is only occasionally put into effect. But Peace Strategy, which has to do with preparation for war, "concerns us all and always"—"Peace Strategy bears the same relation to War Strategy that the armourer who makes the rifle bears to the soldier who uses it" (p2).

In Repington's second Aldershot lecture, The Future Of Army Organisation (delivered on January 27, 1909; meeting chaired by General Smith-Dorrien), he commented that "owing to topsy-turvyness of everything Irish we have done nothing hitherto to create in Ireland the frame-work for our future National Army... However... we shall not be able to say that our National Army is complete until we have achieved the happiness of defending Ireland by Irishmen" (p8).

In the discussion, General Colin Mackenzie said: "We are, Sir, a first-class power and we are apparently looking out for a first-class war". And: "Mr. Haldane's plans for associating the people with the defence of this country is, in my humble opinion, the greatest step that has yet been taken in the organisation of the second line, and history will give this great Scotsman full credit for the measure he has taken... [O]ne of the most interesting and important features of the scheme [Haldane's] is the establishment of a civil organisation for the enrolment of men, and the administration of the Territorial Army. I refer of course tot he County Associations. Their influence... on the country generally ought to be very great, and I feel sure that they will greatly assist the formation of a public opinion on a matter of great public importance, namely that it is only right and just for every man to give to the service of the state that which is given in every other country in Europe... The very fact that Mr. Haldane's scheme is a business-like one, and intended for war, makes them realise how serious is the responsibility which rests on the nation" (p22/3).

In 1911, Repington fed into the new militaristic public opinion of England the idea that the German army was in decay. He did this in a series of articles in The Times on The German Manoeuvres. On October 19th he wrote:

"...the German infantry leaves the impression that the hearts of the men are not in their work. There is nothing in their eyes. The things which one sees in the look of men in a British or a French regiment one seeks in vain in the rather sullen-looking, half-cowed, and machine-made Prussian foot-soldier. The feeling that one receives is that these men are marching and manoeuvring, not because they like it, but because they must, and that without the drive of the corps of officers they would melt away in battle..."

And on October 28th:

"The German Army appears to the writer to have trained itself stale. Year in, year out, the same ceaseless round of intensive training has reduced the whole Army to a machine by which individuality, initiative, and freshness have been rigorously crushed out. The effort to create initiative by regulations has not succeeded. The training... has become a form of somnambulism...

"The world has gone on while Germany has stood still...

"[It is] A Peace-Bred Army...

"No other modern Army displays such profound contempt for the effect of modern fire. [This] can be set down to ignorance and to nothing else...

"...the German Army... appears... to be living on a glorious past and to be unequal to the repute in which it is commonly held...

"The Artillery, with its out-of-date *materiel* and slow and ineffective methods of fire, appeared so inferior that it can have no pretensions to measure itself against the French on anything approaching level terms...

"The iron discipline of the German Army, the strong Imperialism of the well-to-do classes, and the submissiveness of the lower orders, prevent the undermining of military authority by the Socialistic tendencies of large blocks of working people. But in the nation in arms, the Army is the microcosm of the people, and in time of stress the results of Socialistic teaching will not be suppressed to readily as in peace. The character of the German people is greatly changing. The increase of wealth and luxury has an enervating effect upon all classes, and has its reflex action upon the Corps of Officers, which is less simple in its life and tastes and less exclusively professional than it was a score of years ago. Commerce begins to attract the class which has hitherto regarded the Army as the only career open to a gentleman, while in the Army itself there is a steady increase of the non-noble element. The nation, which, after all, gives up little more than half of its able-bodied sons to the service of the Army, is becoming less militarist than formerly...

"Before the patriotic sacrifices of the German people on behalf of its great Army we must all of us incline, and we must never forget that all the living forces of the country will be thrown remorselessly and unsparingly into the furnace of a future war. The totally different conditions which prevail in England, and the puerile belief in the pacific settlement of international disputes which is so pathetically held by good people among us in the face of all the evidence of the times in which we live, must cause us all to spare no efforts to build up year by year more numerous and more efficient forces for the day of trial which may be near at hand.

"But at the same time, should the worst come to the worst, we must also recognise that the German Army is not the wholly perfect machine that it is supposed to be, and that the Triple Entente has much to its credit which, with good statesmanship and good leading, can be turned to the best account.

Bibliography

Archer, W.	Fighting A Philosophy (1914)
Asquith, H.	The Volunteer & Other Poems (1915)
Asquith, H.H.	Memories & Reflections (1928)
	A United Empire (1914)
	The War Of Civilisation (1914)
Casement, R.	The Crime Against Europe (1914)
Childers, E.	The Battle Area In The North Sea (Daily News 8.8.1914)
	The Framework Of Home Rule (1911)
	German Influence On British Cavalry (1911)
	The Riddle Of The Sands (1903)
	The Times History Of The War In South Africa. Vol. V (1907)
	War And The Arme Blanche (1910)
Churchill, W.S.	The World Crisis
Clifford, B.	Connolly Cut-Outs (1984)
	Connolly: The Polish Aspect (1985)
	Derry And The Boyne (1990)
Connolly, J.	A Continental Revolution (Forward 16.8.1914)
	The War Upon The German Nation (Irish Worker 29.8.1914)
	The Workers' Republic (1915-16)
Daily News	(August 1914)
Dicey, A.V.	A Fool's Paradise (1913)
	The Law Of The Constitution (1915 edn)
Doyle, A.C.	The Great Boer War (1900)
	The War In South Africa (1902)
Foster, R.	Modern Ireland (1988)
Freeman's Journal	(July/Sept 1914)
Haldane, R.B.	An Autobiography (1929)
Hansard	(July/Sept 1914)
Harris, Frank	England Or Germany (1915)
Hitler, A.	Mein Kampf
Ireland, J. de C.	Revolutionary Movements Of The Past (1971)

Irish Independent	(August 1914)
Irish News	(July/Sept 1914)
Kettle, T.M.	Battle Songs Of The Irish Brigades (1915)
	Belgium's Cry for Vengeance (Daily News 12.9.1914)
	Europe Against The Barbarians (Daily News 10.8.1914)
	Introduction to Halevy's Life Of Nietzsche (1911)
Lichnowsky, Prince	My London Mission (1918)
Lee, J. Ireland	1912-1988 (1989)
Lynd, R.	Introduction to Connolly, Labour in Ireland (1917)
	World Power Or Downfall: Germany's War Of Conquest (Daily News 10.9.1914)
Manchester Guardian	(August/September 1914)
Martin, F.X.	The Howth Gun Running (1964)
Murray, G.	The Bacchae (translator)
	Thoughts On The War (1914)
Nitti, F.	Peaceless Europe (1921)
O'Connor,T.P.	Irish Heroes In The War (1917)
	Biography Of O'Connor by H. Fyffe (1930)
O'Donnell, C.J.	The Failure Of Lord Curzon (1903)
	The Irish Future (19209)
	The Lordship Of The world (1924)
	The Present Discontents In India (1908)
Repington, Col.	The Future Of Army Organisation (1909)
	The German Army Manoeuvres (The Times, October 1911)
	Peace Strategy (1907)
Seeley, J.R.	The Expansion Of England (1882)
Shaw, G.B.	Common Sense About The War (1914)
Spender, H.	H.H. Asquith (1915)

Index

Adams, F. 98
Agadir 50
Agricola 92
Albrecht, Duke 79
Aldershot Military Society 108
Alsace 43, 83
Algeciras Conference 52
All-for-Ireland League 8
America 46
Andries, General 10
Angel, N. 74
Anglo-Celts 17, 18
Anglo-Irish Agreement 19
A.O.H. 24, 30, 43
Antrim 36
Archer, W. 25
Arnold, M. 106
Asgard 16
Ashbourne, Lord 16
Asquith, H. 100
Asquith, Margot 56, 82, 84
Asquith, H.H. 5, 6, 8, 17, 19, 22, 32, 33, 35, 37-40, 42-3, 52-5, 57, 60, 65-6, 69, 72, 82-3, 87, 103-5
Asquith R. 82
Austria 5, 6, 42, 57
Athenaeum 21

Bachelor's Walk 16
Baden-Baden 63
Balance of Power 56, 85
Balfour, A.J. 19, 53, 82
Barclay, T. 70
Belfast 14, 24
Belgium 18, 24, 50-1, 58, 75-8, 82, 84, 95
Belloc, H. 78
Benedict, Pope XV 81-2
Bengal 47
Bennet, A. 29
Bennett, J. 75

Berkley, G. F. 16
Bernhardi, General 24, 26-7
Bethmann Hollweg 58
Bezel, Lt. Col. 62
Bible 22-3
Birkenhead, Lord 52, 84
Bismarck 53, 59
Blücher, Marshal 59
Boer War 9-13, 17, 19, 61, 71, 76
Bolshevism 20, 29
Bonar Law 31, 41-2
Botha 61
Brandes, G. 25
Bryce, Lord 75
Buat, General 50, 62
Burnet, G. 18
Burns, J. 32
Bury, Rev. H. 64
Butt, I. 64

Caldwell, C.E. 49
Callaghan, Admiral 43
Cambridge 12, 18
Cambron 56
Camden Town 20-1
Campbell-Bannerman, H. 8-9, 19, 52, 83, 85
Canada 59
Cape Colony 10
Carlyle, T. 18
Carndonagh 47
Carson, E. 9, 36, 42, 47, 52, 56, 59, 84
Carthage 23, 92
Casement, R. 5, 9, 16, 20, 87-92, 99
Catholic-nationalism 23
Cavalry 12-14
Chartism 21
Childers, E. 9-16, 26, 88
China 71-2
Chinese Empire 86

Cholah 16
Christian Socialists 20-1
Christianity 27-8
Churchill, W.S. 8-9, 19, 33, 39, 43, 47, 50-2, 55-8, 62, 65-6, 70, 83-5, 104-5
Clausewitz 87-8
Cobb, I.S. 75
Communist Party 98
Concentration Camps 10-13
Congo 89
Connolly, J. 5, 92-9
Contemporary Review 74
Copenhagen 76
Cork 8, 14, 20, 24, 27, 35, 61
Cowen, J. 9, 45
Cox, H. 70
Cramb, M. 96
Cromwell 21
Crowe, E. 65, 71-2
Curragh Mutiny 38-9
Curzon, Lord 47

D'Abernon, Lord 72
Daily News 24, 26, 33, 38, 42
Daily Mail 43, 75-9
Daily Telegraph 78
Darwinism 27-8, 30
Davis, R.H. 78
Davitt, M. 83
Dawe, A.J. 78
Delcassé, M. 53, 57, 71
Devlin, J. 24, 43, 83
Dicey, A.V. 7, 21, 29
Dilke, C. 62
Dillon, J. 30, 83
Donegal 47
Douglas, Lord A. 85
Down, Co. 49
Doyle, A.C. 17-19
Dublin 5, 19, 24, 42-3

Easter Rising 6, 83, 86-7, 100
Echo de Paris 79
Edinburgh 5
Edinburgh Review 72
Egypt 84, 90
English Christianity 22
Eton 59
Eucken, R. 96
Euripedes 107
Evening Standard 25

Fascism 29
Fenians 16
Fermanagh 34
Figgis, D. 16
Fisher, Lord 80
Fitt, Lord 23
Fitzgerhald, Ald. 45
Flanders 5
Fleet Street 12
Foch, Marshal 76
Fontenoy 59
Fortescue 59
Foster, R. 99
Fox, C.J. 37
France 27, 29, 43, 50-62, 70, 72, 74, 84-5, 89-90, 92
Franco-German War 83
Frankfort 63
Frederick the Great 27
Freeman's Journal 33, 35-7, 40-1
Free Trade 14, 19
Freiburg 63
French, Field Marshal 51, 57
Fyfe, H. 9, 47

Gaelic Ireland 20
Garvin, J.L. 49
German Philosophy 23, 65
Gilbert, M. 75
Gladstone 16-20, 32-3,

39, 50-1, 62, 88
Glasgow 45
Globe, The 79
Grattan, H. 33
Greater Britain 18
Greece 23
Grenfell, Lord 80
Grattan's Parliament
Green, A.S. 16
Grey, E. 6, 8-9, 17, 19, 30, 32-3, 39, 42, 50, 52, 53-6, 69, 84-5, 87, 103, 105
Gwynn, S. 44, 97

Haldane, R.B. 8, 17, 19, 21-2, 33, 38-9, 51-4, 56, 62, 65, 69, 85, 87, 108
Hanson, H. 75
Hardinge, Lord 54
Harmsworth 43
Harris, A. 63
Harris, F. 106
Harrison, F. 21
Heine, H. 106
Heinemann 25
Hitler, A. 28
Hobhouse, E. 11
Holmes, S. 19
Hume, J. 19
Hun, The 26
Huns 78

ILP 92
Imperial Federation 19
India 18, 47, 51, 54, 84
Inge, Dean 65, 74
Ireland, J. de C. 98-9
Irish Brigade 5, 40, 44-5
Irish Independent 33, 44
Irish News 3506, 41-3
I.R.A. 23, 49
Irish Unionist Party 14
Irish University Bill 47
Irish Volunteers 16, 24
Isvolsky 53
Italy 28, 76

Jacobite 45
Japan 58
Jameson 61
Jesus 18

Kaiser, The 11, 24-6, 35-7, 43, 52, 55, 57-8, 60, 69, 74
Keenan, J. 18
Kelpie 16
Kettle, T.M. 24-5, 29-30, 44-5, 98
Keynes, J.M. 18
Kiel REgatta 85
Kipling, R. 26, 74
Kitchener, Lord 12-3, 43, 76
Kruger, P. 61, 71

Land & Labour 14
Lascelles, F. 5
Latapie, M. 82
Lawrence, A. 16
Lee, J. 99-100
Lenin 27, 93, 96
Lewis, R. 75
Liberal Imperialism 6, 8-9, 11-12, 15-7, 19-21, 32-4, 38, 48-9, 58, 71, 87
Liberal Party 7-8, 33, 38-9
Liberal Unionism 7, 16-7, 19, 21
Lichnowsky, Prince 6
Liverpool 45
Lloyd George 13, 42, 49, 56, 69
Logue, Cardinal 79
Londonderry, Lord 6
Lorraine 43, 83
Louvain 78
Locke, J. 18
Lucan, Cardinal 79
Lusitania 46
Lynd, R, 26, 29, 97-8

Mackenzie, Gen. C. 109
MacMahon, General 78

Erratum
Page 13: Kitchenette
should read Kitchener

ATHOL BOOKS DISTRIBUTION SERVICE

"The Labour Opposition" Of Northern Ireland, Introduced by Joe
Keenan. Reprint of entire run of this Belfast paper of 1925/6, Athol Books, 1992,
ISBN 0 85034 054 3

The Origin Of Irish Catholic-Nationalism. Selections from Walter Cox's
"Irish Magazine": 1807-1815, Introduced and Edited by Brendan
Clifford, Athol Books, ISBN 0 85034 53 5

The Economics Of Partition A Historical Survey Of Ireland In Terms Of Political
Economy, by Brendan Clifford, Athol Books, ISBN 0 85034 056 X

"Godless Colleges" And Mixed Education In Ireland Extracts from Speeches
and Writings of Thomas Wyse, Daniel O'Connell, Thomas Davis, Charles Gavan
Duffy, Frank Hugh O'Donnell and Others. Introduced andEdited by Angela
Clifford Athol Books, ISBN 0 85034 056 X

Irish Education: The Case For Secular Reform by David Alvey
*Preface by Michael D. Higgins, TD. Experiences of the system, the facts and figures,
historical appendices.* Church & State Books and Athol Books, 1991, ISBN 0 85034
047 0

Faith And Fatherland by Fr. Pat Buckley
The Irish News, The Catholic Hierarchy And The Management Of Dissidents
Belfast Historical &Educational Society, 1991, ISBN 1 872078 02 8
The Veto Controversy by Brendan Clifford
Including Thomas Moore's Letter To The Roman Catholics Of Dublin (1810).
Athol Books, 1985, ISBN 0 85034 030 6
Scripture Politics by Rev. William Steel Dickson, *The Most Influential United Irishman Of The North.* Introduced and edited by Brendan Clifford. Athol Books, 1991, ISBN 0 85034 044 6
Billy Bluff And The Squire (A Satire On Irish Aristocracy) by Rev. James Porter, *who was hanged in the course of the United Irish Rebellion of 1798.* Introduced and edited by Brendan Clifford. Athol Books, 1991, ISBN 0 85034 045 4
The Causes Of The Rebellion In Ireland by Rev. Thomas Ledlie Birch, *who was exiled after being courtmartialed during the rebellion of 1798.* Introduced and edited by Brendan Clifford. Athol Books, 1991, ISBN 085034 046 2
Belfast In The French Revolution by Brendan Clifford
Extracts from the United Irish paper, the Northern Star. Belfast Historical & Educational Society, 1989, ISBN 1 872078 00 1
Thomas Russell And Belfast by Brendan Clifford. *Account of 18th Belfast and of "The Man From God Knows Where". Extracts from Russell's Journal, and his satire, Lion Of Old England,* Athol Books, 1988, ISBN 085034 033 0
Derry And The Boyne by Nicholas Plunket. *A Contemporary Account of The Siege Of Derry, The Battle Of The Boyne and The General Condition Of Ireland In the Jacobite War.* Introduced by Brendan Clifford. Belf. Hist. & Educ. Soc. ISBN 1 872078 01 X
The O'Neill Years by David Gordon
Unionist Politics 1963-1969. Athol Books, 1989, ISBN 085034 039 X
From Civil Rights To National War by Pat Walsh
Northern Ireland Catholics Politics 1964-74. Athol Books, 1989, ISBN 085034 040 3
Northern Ireland And The Algerian Analogy: A Suitable Case For Gaullism? by Hugh Roberts. Critique of colon theory. Athol Books, 1986, ISBN 085034 031 4
The Constitutional History Of Eire/Ireland by Angela Clifford
Post-1921 Constitutional developments, set in their political context. Athol Books, 1987, ISBN 085034 032 2
The Life And Poems Of Thomas Moore by Brendan Clifford
Athol Books, 1984, ISBN 085034 029 9
The Dubliner: The Lives, Times And Writings Of James Clarence Magan by Brendan Clifford. Athol Books, 1988, ISBN 085034 036 5
A Story Of The Armada by Captrain Francisco De Cuellar, Joe Keenan and others. *Additional material by Madawc Williams, Pope Sixtus the Fifth and Admiral Monson.* Athol Books (for Bel. Hist. & Educ. Soc.), 1988, ISBN 085034 037 3
Poor Law In Ireland by Angela Clifford. *Historical review starting in 1838, detailed account of 1932 Outdoor Relief Dispute, refutation of Paddy Devlin's book on subject.* Athol Books, 1983, ISBN 085034 033 0 (a 163-page, A4 pamphlet)

All the books are available, by mail order only, from:

Athol Books,

10 Athol Street, Belfast, BT12 4GX
SEND FOR A FULL CATALOGUE